EARLY PRAISE

"David Feela is a poet, fiction writer, and essayist and in *Feelasophy* he brings all those strengths to bear: precise and lyrical language, excellent storytelling, and exactitude of focus and argument. I thoroughly enjoyed reading this book and will keep it near for travels, camping trips, long open afternoons, and moments when I need quick inspiration. As 'they' say, you're gonna love it."

—DAVID LEE, former Utah poet laureate and author of *Rusty Barbed Wire*

"David Feela's essays are funny, poignant, and profound. His observations of everyday life, history, and literature make a quick and easy read, yet they linger in your mind long after you put down the book. He notices the wry and amusing aspects of simple things the rest of us take for granted. It was a great pleasure to read every word of *Feelasophy*."

—GAIL BINKLY, author of *Trek of a Bird-Woman*

"David Feela's delightful new collections invites you into a world that is at once comical and rich with meaning. His observations range from the seemingly insignificant—the half-life of a light bulb, a discarded high school ring—to the profound and transcendent. He squeezes wisdom out of everyday moments, whether shopping for groceries or purchasing a truly cheesy souvenir T-shirt. In the traditions of Mark Twain and Kurt Vonnegut, these essays illuminate the often-overlooked landscape of American popular culture. They also hold up a mirror that allows us to recognize ourselves—and then sometimes laugh out loud."

—BILL MEISSNER, author of *The Wonders of the Little World*

"David Feela is a funny man with a poet's eye for detail and a keen sense of the ridiculous. His writing is infused with good cheer and humor. He likes puns and isn't afraid to use them. *Feelasophy* is informed by his love of words and his delight in playing with them. All the better for his readers, as he takes us down the quirky and offbeat backroads of life."

—PETER ANDERSON, author of *Riding the Wheel*

Feelasophy

y

SAY YES QUICKLY BOOKS

Scottsdale, Arizona USA

The essays included in this collection were first published in the *Denver Post*, *Durango Telegraph*, *Four Corners Free Press*, and *High Country News*.

Cover watercolor by P. Smith.

Author photograph by Pam Smith.

ISBN: 978-1-965342-04-6

First print edition.

Feelasophy

selected essays
DAVID FEELA

ALSO BY DAVID FEELA

Little Acres
So Delicate These Arches
The Home Atlas
Thought Experiments

Once again, this book is dedicated to Pam, who reads me like a book with her whole heart and mind

"Keep Calm and Carry On"

—1939 British motivational poster

CONTENTS

PREFACE

At first glance, I thought the letters "CNF" might belong on the side of a semi-trailer truck, but acronyms are like that. In their need to be brief, the meaning gets lost. You have to live with them in some kind of context before any legitimate meaning pops into your head. When I finally understood that CNF is an acronym for "creative nonfiction," I had the context I needed. After all, I've been writing it for decades. Now, I recognize CNF for what it is to me, and for the ways in which it defines my own approach to writing.

Creative nonfiction is nonfiction all dressed up in its Sunday best. Both forms depend on facts to inform the reader. The most obvious distinction between them is that creative nonfiction employs fiction writers' tools to tell fact-based stories—and it *is* possible to write factually *and* creatively. All good journalists do so all the time. In my own essays, I use figurative devices like scene setting, metaphor, dialogue, and even character development in my attempts to bring my stories, my essays to life, and the main character in virtually all of the essays in this book is me.

Forty years ago, my wife Pam and I moved from Minnesota to the southwest corner of Colorado, in the Four Corners region, where I accepted a job teaching advanced placement English, speech, and creative writing to high-school students. That thousand-mile move led to a *feelasophical* shift in my awareness of surroundings, people, and cultures, the likes of which I had never experienced before.

In the classroom, ideas crowded into my life like the students who bounded in every weekday. I assigned "serious" literature, but I spiced it up with as many puns and jokes as I could squeeze into the minutes before the bell rang. My students' curiosity fueled me. Their confusion prompted explanations. And we learned from one another. So, if "philosophy" is the study of the fundamental nature of knowledge, reality, and existence, then "feelasophy" must mean more of the same but with a bit of a personal touch.

If you have not encountered my first book of essays, *How Delicate These Arches*—once a finalist for the Colorado Book Award in, yes, creative nonfiction—I recommend it. This new book, *Feelasophy*, amounts to a second offering of essays my first volume sought to explore, offering readers explorations, excursions, and insights into matters illuminated by the land and people living in the American West—and occasionally far beyond.

It's a book that I hope will energize you with new information and new perspectives. And I hope that it will sometimes urge you to smile. By now, I have retired from teaching, so *Feelasophy* is what we used to call "free reading." It's not an assignment, and I promise you won't be tested.

1: YOU THOUGHT YOU'D SEE THE WORLD

THOUGHTS ON TOURISM

If René Descartes traveled extensively during the seventeenth century like today's tourists do, he might never have written, "I think, therefore I am," but instead might have chosen an axiom like, "I see, therefore I be." As a philosopher whose explorations were confined to the hemispheres of his brain, Descartes understood little about the tourism industry, and it's likely he never would have approved of this syllogism that explains a contemporary phenomenon: the souvenir T-shirt. All tourists pack clothing and some of the packed clothing includes T-shirts. Therefore, all tourists buy T-shirts. I own a favorite from a trip I took along Route 66 that says, "Standin' On the Corner, Winslow, Arizona." I also bought one with the image of a ukulele that proclaims, "Hawaii Lifestyle." I'm not sure what that means, but I loved the shade of green that reminded me of Kauai where I visited for one very rainy week. I earned it, whatever *it* means. It stands as my hundred-percent cotton declaration that, "I was there."

When a person travels, the urge to preserve the exotic and serendipitous experience supersedes the mind's natural tendency to classify the day as, say, just another Friday. Tourists eat, drink, take pictures, read travel brochures and maps, and they find places to sleep. Sure, these activities can be done at home much less expensively, but traveling excites the "what the hell" gene and a tourist accepts absurdity as if it were an omen.

And a $30 T-shirt? Sure, that's a bargain. Books like *1,000 Places to See Before You Die* only highlight my fear of never being able to travel enough, especially if I take the book's premise seriously, and that my ultimate self-awareness and fulfillment lies in a bucket list of recommended vacation destinations. My other worry is that I'll end up with a dresser drawer stuffed with T-shirts, more than I could possibly wear for the rest of my life.

Then again, my homebody-self suspects something must be wrong with people who travel. Backed as I am into the Four Corners, brewing my own coffee and paying for internet access, I know T-shirts are less expensive than round trip plane tickets.

You see, I'm caught between these deep blue seas. One part of me wants to explore—to see the Eiffel Tower, the ruins of Pompeii, to float in a Venetian gondola—while the other is so grateful to finally get home, he can't imagine what drove him away in the first place. Then, from the bottom of my suitcase a soiled souvenir T-shirt surfaces. I unfold it—this pledge to be a tourist—and drape it like a flag over my chest.

Descartes believed that thought—not our senses—turns us into human beings. We hear, taste, touch, even see the world like any other creature, but only by being aware of our perceptions do we become (and here I take a liberty) tourists. I know, the money collected from travelers by local economies is appreciated, but like philosophers, tourists don't get respect.

Descartes also postulated that the untrustworthiness of the senses can be illustrated by his Wax Argument. It goes like this: one's senses perceive the wax's chunkiness, but if you set it over a flame, a transformation renders the senses senseless. Like a paramedic arriving on the scene of an accident, thought rescues us and returns us to our—dare I say it again?—senses. Stay at home too long and my life begins to feel like wax but leave home and I notice how travel alters me. In the fire of the world's strangeness, I glimpse the alchemy of a moment, pure gold.

That's probably enough philosophy. Born with a *fee-lasopher*'s moniker, I can't help going mental once in a while, which is why I value the souvenir T-shirt, because it weaves the fleeting nature of my travel experiences into the physicality of my daily life. It's that simple. It allows me to carry each personal transformation close to my skin, to wash it and fold it and tell an occasional story about my latest trip whenever an unsuspecting stranger asks me about my T-shirt.

I've considered a trip to Prague for my next meta-morphosis, visiting the Kafka museum, but I've always wanted to visit Gibraltar too, a British dependency at the southern tip of the Iberian peninsula. It usually takes me a full year to muster the courage for another major assault on my sedentary senses, but it helps to imagine myself coming home with a souvenir T-shirt, something with the picture of cockroach, say, or better yet,

Gibraltar Rocks!

LIFE BEHIND THE CURTAIN

T hings happen on airplanes for reasons, although not all of them are obvious, discernible, or even reasonable.

Take, for example, the curtain between first class and economy sections on a commercial airliner, which is intended to fool first-class passengers into believing that the back half of the airplane isn't tagging along behind them. Then there are the tiny scratched-but-certified-shatterproof plastic windows at opposite ends of each seat row, as if a view rationally explains how traveling at 550 miles per hour, 39,000 feet above the surface of the earth is normal. And while I'm chronicling the crazy, try convincing any sane passenger that by slipping on a little yellow rubber inflatable life vest and blowing into a red tube, a person might stay afloat, much less alive, in a sea of disaster.

A version of modern mythology must be embraced by passengers when they climb aboard an airplane, but even more disturbing is that airlines have manipulatively embraced the notion they can not only sell these myths, but that services ought to be dispensed by the pound or by the inch.

Anyone who has flown today's less-than-friendly skies can't help noticing the ironic "handy hints" provided by the airline to keep passengers feeling fit while en-route to their destinations, like rotating one's foot in one direction, then in the other fifteen times, raising the leg and tensing the muscles of the thigh thirty times. A bit idiotic really, because it's the same airline that eliminated the space to safely perform even these minimalist exercises they're so prudently recommending. Try doing the "back and arms" stretcher fifteen times by bending forward and moving your hands down to your legs as the passenger in front of you slams his seat backward against your skull.

On a recent trip to Italy, I confess, I purchased an upgrade—economy *plus*. I'd inquired about the upgrade at the check-in desk. Business class? Sure, why not? I am, after all, a writer. The cost? An additional $1,360! That's more than the total price of my ticket! Oh, economy *plus* is only $100 more. Sure, I'll take that.

By paying an additional $100 for legroom near the front of the cabin where the plane manufacturer was forced to install a wall, the airline assured me I'd be able to "see what other travelers are talking about" and to "savor more space to work and relax." It may have been the word "savor" that tipped the scale for me. I hadn't eaten anything since breakfast. All I know is that I'd never paid for anything so extravagant before in my touristing life. I figured the splurge cost me about $20 an inch.

I stuck with the standard economy class on the return flight, but I'd lucked out and been assigned an aisle seat. From that vantage, I noticed an attendant pausing on her way toward the front of the cabin and glancing down at a passenger. She crouched very low, like a kindergarten teacher talking meaningfully to a toddler, and made gestures toward her own eyes. Another cabin attendant approached from the other direction and some sort of secret conference transpired until one attendant walked away, returning shortly with a plastic glass filled with a cloudy liquid. The passenger drank it, both attendants watched, talked a bit more, then the miraculous event occurred.

The passenger was invited to join the other passengers in the first-class cabin, and the entire delegation disappeared behind the gold curtain.

As I glanced down toward my feet, thinking about the futility of touching them for the next three hours, I noticed a tiny paper bag in the pouch between the glossy airline marketing magazine and the instruction card for emergencies. I pulled it free and read the label: sickness bag.

So, this is what it takes, I thought—barfing into a paper bag—to make an airline measure out an ounce of compassion. I opened the bag and stared into it. The woman next to me seemed to be vigorously trying to rotate her shoulders in a circular motion—at least five times. Good for her.

The whole idea of packing people like cattle into an airplane, and then charging them additional fees to be treated like human beings sickened me, but it was not enough to produce anything, well, let's just say, meaningful. I folded the paper bag and placed it back into its pouch.

After all, the beverage service was about to begin. The wheeled cart had just appeared from behind the curtain. Like Dorothy from the Wizard of Oz, I'd seen enough to realize the entire performance was a sham, but seriously, my mouth tasted like dust and I needed something to drink.

HOW TO MAKE A MALTESE CROSS

The bus driver was in a foul mood, shouting out the window in broken English, "Whadda ya want?" when I politely inquired if his bus went to Rabat. He turned away from me, perhaps nodding his head, perhaps not, and examined his fingernails. I'd watched him curse a pigeon for landing near his bus prior to asking for information.

We were, after all, just tourists on his island, and it was our first attempt at using Malta's notorious fleet of yellow buses. According to our guidebook, the buses will get you anywhere on the island. According to our driver, questions will get you nowhere.

Pam travels with me because she doesn't get flustered easily. She turned to a passenger standing on the loading platform and asked, "Does this bus go to Rabat?" and when he nodded she asked how much fare is required.

In my version of an Un-Lonely Planet travel guide, I would advise readers to always travel with a companion, preferably one that comes up smelling like roses every time you step in the dog pile.

We took our seats only a few rows from the door, afraid to miss our stop. Without warning, without so much as the door closing, the bus lurched to life. We hung on tightly to the seat in front of us, nearly spilled into the aisle by the cornering as we headed out of the roundabout and into traffic. We'd accomplished our travel goal for the day: trying something unusual. If we survived, we'd try for a more pedestrian goal tomorrow, like walking.

Some of the old buses still in operation were manufactured in the 1950s, and all are painted a bright yellow, often with pin-striping and hand-lettered messages across the fenders like, *Thank God*, or *Life in Heaven*. Nearly every bus has an inspirational picture of Jesus or the Virgin Mary prominently displayed inside, often on the panel just above the driver's head. The Maltese are mostly Catholic and their devotion to the church is perhaps justified by scaring the hell out of so many tourists.

After our breakneck start, the driver picked up more passengers on the way out of town. I was impressed by every passenger's consideration for older folks, always moving toward the back of the bus to allow, say, a little old lady a convenient front seat. Pam tapped me on the shoulder to point out an older man who'd just boarded, paid his fare, and then made the sign of the cross immediately as he seated himself—no doubt, a kind of spiritual self-defense. The bus lurched forward again, and we cleared the crowded streets of Valletta, Malta's capital city, without crushing any tiny vehicles weaving in and out of the lanes of traffic.

Deep down, every Maltese motorist desires to be a bus driver. The roads are so narrow I still have trouble believing two buses moving in opposite directions pass without scraping paint. Outside the city, we settled back to watch the countryside open up like the pages of a picture book, miles of the island's rock walls and terraced fields, cactus hedges and sixteenth-century limestone buildings, inducing a trance that made me forget the oncoming traffic.

It must have been a deep trance, because suddenly the bus braked so hard we were lifted from our seats into a standing position. The driver hit the horn as if the little town of Zebbug formed the new walls of Jericho, a virtual canyon of tenements on both sides of the bus he wanted to reduce to rubble. The horn blared, nonstop, echoing off the stone. I could see through the windshield that nobody occupied any of the cars parked along the street, but he may have planned to move them by the sheer force of decibels.

We waited five minutes, our ears ringing, when from behind a tiny doorway a young woman emerged, hurrying toward the offending cars. She jumped into one of them, started it up, and pulled away. The bus took off, and now we were seriously making up for lost time. At the next town we stood to exit with a clutch of other passengers. I suspected it might be Rabat, but I wasn't going to ask. I did, however, thank the driver before exiting. "Whadda for?" he shouted at me, one hand poised in the air like a priest at the end of a benediction. What could I say? We'd been blessed.

HEDGING

The Irish call them "The Dark Hedges," and perhaps they once resembled hedges when James Stuart's family first planted 150 beech trees along the avenue leading to their newly constructed eighteenth-century Gracehill House. Had he been born a century later in the American West, he'd likely have settled for an imposing structure of log pillars at the entrance to his property.

The sign swinging from a crosspiece would have christened his acreage "Grace Ranch" and I'd be uninspired, without anything else to write.

Luckily over two hundred years have passed, filling a gap in my imagination. Stuart's narrow strip of "hedges," intended to impress his neighbors, are now overseen by the Heritage Trust. The compact landmark stands in stark contrast to the vast national park vistas America offers its visitors, like a tiny luminescent pearl in the history of northern Ireland.

Tour busses pass through the tunnel under the trees, then pull over just beyond it. Passengers disembark with cameras and swarm across the road surface, desperate for the perfect selfie or an inspired scenic photograph. I should know, I was one of them, but I also witnessed a woman nearly run over by an oncoming vehicle. Enchantments can prove risky.

A sudden squall of rain sent everyone running for cover. I captured my photo gem—just the trees—veiled in mist and shimmering in the stormy light. Before stopping the bus, speaking into his microphone, the driver warned everyone, twice, about the danger of standing on the road for the sake of taking photos without paying attention to traffic. But the setting proved too irresistible, and not just for amateur photographers. HBO also made the location famous by featuring it as "the King's Road" in its popular series *Game of Thrones,* which explains why more and more fans from around the globe travel to see how magically the light intersects with the latticework of limbs and leaves.

I returned to the bus. The driver laughed as I stepped inside, wiping the rain from my face. He explained how the increasing number of visitors are transforming the hedges into a traffic hazard, and that tour buses might soon be required to register for a time slot if choosing to travel along the Bregagh Road.

"But the trees," I said, "are so beautiful."

"Aye," he replied, "but it's the population that can't control its girth. Only ninety trees remain. They should be the protected ones."

Eventually the sun peeked through the clouds as the green countryside rolled past our bus windows. The driver spoke again to his captive audience about a different tree in northern Ireland called the Fairy Thorn, also referred to as fairy bushes, which are really native hawthorns. Unlike beech trees, they tend to grow like hermits, in the middle of fields, on wind-blown rocky terrains, or at the crown of small hills. According to legend, one of their enchantments is to offer a safe habitat for the wee folk.

It's also a national disgrace to harm them. Just try to cut one down and your axe handle will split, your chainsaw will sputter, the engine of your bulldozer will seize. Try poison and you'll wake up feeling like you've been gut-shot. Stories about unsuccessful tree removals have been passed down for generations.

One tree, an ancient fairy bush, has been growing at the Ormeau Golf Club since 1893, when the course first opened. Greenskeepers reportedly will not touch it or even trim it. If a golf ball hits it, the Irish don't curse. Apologize to the tree, golfers say, and at least you won't be given a bad game.

Many Irish believe in the power the wee folk wield to help the big ones. A tree might be discovered in the middle of nowhere, already adorned with ribbons and strips of material torn from the clothing of the sick or suffering. These offerings are not motivated by any fear of what harm the fairies might conjure, but in the sincere hope these spirits might help heal them.

Our driver promised to take his passengers to see a Fairy Thorn and I could feel a tremor of excitement ripple through the bus. As we approached a curve in the road, sure enough, a small tree just off the road stood festooned with a flurry of fluttering ribbons. He slowed the bus for the sake of the cameras.

"Can't we stop for a closer look?" someone shouted from the back of the bus.

By way of an answer he stepped on the gas. Either the heavy side-traffic on this narrow road prompted his quick departure or he knew what the fairies could do to a busload of tourists trampling the turf where they reside. Either way, he probably saved lives.

KAUAI-IT

A couple we know sat down at a local coffee shop and told us of their excellent trip to Kauai, one of the Hawaiian islands which offers to tourists—among many pleasures—more than nine-thousand acres of coffee beans. They mentioned the beautiful Nepali coast, the exceptional "Little Grand Canyon," snorkeling with turtles, cascading waterfalls, lush tropical vegetation, and of course relaxing on a multitude of white sand beaches. They never mentioned the chickens.

Like the cows of India, feral chickens roam the island under what must be a protected sacred status among its residents. The birds are everywhere, clucking and crowing, scratching in the gravel along the roads, along hedgerows, and laying their eggs in the ruff beside all the manicured greens at every resort golf course. They show up in parking lots to dodge impatient motorists, strut beside the beaches, and they're usually hanging out in clutches of a half-dozen or more *gangs* of chickens, rousing quite a few hackles with their chicken language.

The idea that roosters only crow to greet the morning sun—a sort of rural early riser's alarm clock—is a myth. For ten days outside our window, although it sounded close enough to be broadcast from under our bed, hours before any inkling of dawn, two menacing gangs had their lead roosters rehearse what I can only describe as a poorly acted version of *West Side Story*. They continued the performances until dawn, and often beyond.

Island folklore excuses the chorus and rationalizes the plentitude of chickens by praising their toughness. It says, for instance, that if a person boiled a chicken in a pot with a lava rock, the rock would come out the more tender. I just don't see any evidence to prove the theory has been sufficiently tested.

My wife's nephew told us another mythic tale about the rise of the wild chicken, spinning the story that during early island history some chickens were considered sacred and some were simply domestic stock, but a storm loosed them from their confines and the caste system was broken.

Because no one could be certain which chickens were sacred and which were to be served up for dinner, the people of Kauai elected not to eat any of these free-ranging chickens. He told us this story while consuming a Hawaiian chicken pizza at a local restaurant, a smile on his face nearly as wide as his pizza slice.

An appetite for cockfighting may also have prompted all the current chicken trouble. Filipinos supposedly introduced brightly colored fighting cocks to breed with the Walla, the wild chickens. In this version of good and evil, like the snake in the Garden of Eden, the rooster must be held accountable for all the Garden Isle's ills.

In 1863, Mark Twain lectured in New York about his visit to the Sandwich Islands (which is how people referred to Hawaii in the nineteenth century). He joked about the natives' dietary habits, boasting that they "are very hospitable, and feast their guests on roast dog and fricasseed cat." I'll admit, I counted very few cats—the few I did see looking very feeble and mangy—and all the dogs taken for walks appeared well-fed and on leashes, all of them under stern instruction to avoid direct eye contact with the chickens. However the birds increased in number to a population that equals or (as some say) exceeds the 65,000 residents of the island, the truth is that the birds have virtually no predators, isolated as they are within a tropical 562-square-mile coop by that beautiful blue expanse of the Pacific Ocean.

The most serious threat to their livelihood is, perhaps, a tourist rental car. I saw a few fatalities flattened against the pavement, although there was no way to tell if the feathered speedbumps were the result of accidents or premeditated *poultry-cide* committed by temporarily insane, sleep-deprived guests on the island.

I've heard all the explanations, and the most reasonable one I encountered for the plethora of chickens blames Hurricane Iniki in 1992, a fowl wind that unleashed and scattered the island's feathered stock. And because birds tend to understand wind, their survival at least seems plausible. Just do the math: twenty years + unrestrained cock-a-doodle-doing = a bevy of chicks.

In the end, I prefer cows to chickens, which is why I returned to rural Montezuma County, Colorado. I'll never live in a tropical paradise. And besides, I'm not a fan of Spam, a product which Hawaiians consume in greater quantities than any other State in the Union. Why is Spam so popular in Hawaii? If you ask me, it's because it sits in a can on the shelf, so quietly.

STOP AND GO

As I checked in at a hotel on Calypso's island, a receptionist secretly pushed a little button below her desk and a waiter appeared, carrying a chilled glass of orange juice to the desk.

"Is that for me?"

"Yes, compliments of the hotel." This was the first of several ploys to keep me as a guest. I'd have thought discounting the room price for a vacationing tourist would have been more effective, and I should have complained, but I didn't.

According to legend, the Greek goddess Calypso kept Odysseus a prisoner for seven years on this very island in the Mediterranean. Supposedly she was beautiful, and she could transform her beauty to suit any man's desire.

Just my luck. I got orange juice. But then again, I'd only planned on staying overnight. Calypso had access to a wide array of powerful spells and unlimited wealth; I was traveling on a budget. My limited itinerary included dinner, a stroll along the beach, a good night's sleep, and then in the morning a hike to visit Calypso's cave.

Gozo is one of the two sister islands which make up the archipelago nation of Malta, just south of Sicily. It contains far more cultural, artistic, and natural treasures than any tourist could see in a single day, including temples older than the pyramids, medieval churches, exotic isolated beaches, and many examples of old-world architecture.

"Calypso's cave is part of the Homeric mythology, right?"

"That's right." The receptionist knew her classical literature.

"So the cave is a mythical place?"

She avoided my eyes. "Like gossip, myth originates with a kernel of truth." I'd found the cave listed on a map I picked up while completing the ferry crossing. How mythical locations end up on tourist maps is a logical problem I would have to work out in my spare time once I returned home, but for now, I had an eight-mile hike planned for daybreak, already orienting itself in my mind.

I dropped my bag in the room and returned to the lobby, planning to set off in search of a restaurant. The heat of the late afternoon hit me like a wet towel as

I stepped out the door. I stopped and reconsidered whether I wanted to sweat a slimy trail like a slug along the sidewalk, searching for an attractive place to eat. The receptionist slipped off her perch behind the desk and came up behind me.

"We have an excellent restaurant in the hotel, if you'd care to join us for dinner." The suggestion was a no-brainer. The swelter of the spring Mediterranean sun itched against my chest like an invisible hair-shirt. I turned around and the receptionist led me to a beautiful and cool dining room where a waiter escorted me to a table. I perused the menu he offered, ordered the special and a carafe of the house wine.

While he was gone, I stared into the clear water of an aquarium mounted like a porthole in the wall beside me. I could see the other side of the dining room which appeared slightly out of proportion, like looking through a funhouse mirror, until a large freshwater fish I couldn't identify swam up to hover and stare at me from its side of the glass. We commiserated about our status as trapped beings. I felt comforted because *Homo sapiens* did not appear as an entree on the menu.

My meal was fabulous, although I felt bad about eating sea bass so close to a relative looking on, so I decided to retire to my room, take a long shower, and call it a day.

In the morning I ordered room service. The knock on my door was accompanied by a gentle voice announcing my coffee had arrived. The young woman bringing me breakfast was breathtaking. I couldn't believe how her tresses cascaded over her shoulders or the Mediterranean blue of her eyes. I held the door wide as the sea itself and she placed a silver tray on a black marble table. I should have asked, "How much do I owe you?" but I was afraid she'd say, "Seven years," so I simply nodded and smiled, as if I didn't speak any language, as if I was afflicted by stupidity, as if I was too old to care.

But I'm not the kind of guy who doesn't appreciate an epic. I've studied Odysseus's journey, his twenty years away from home, and his so-called suffering at the hands of his nymph. I sighed. My bed last night radiated such softness it stirred my dreams like the surf crashing below my balcony.

On this island of Gozo there's a cave which my tour book describes as "just a narrow opening near the top of a steep cliff," and as she stooped to pour the coffee I saw where all the trouble began.

THE BOOK OF FOLLY

"The highest form of bliss is living with a certain degree of folly." —Erasmus

Quite a few years ago we traveled to Malta for a two-week holiday, the same year two Libyan pilots defected and landed their jet fighters there, refusing the Libyan military's orders to bomb its protestors. The year we booked a trip to Sicily, Mount Etna erupted in the news with yet another "dangerous" period of volcanic activity. Last year, deciding to play it safe, we visited the UK for an entire month, a nation where we could at least speak the language. Seven days after we arrived, the queen died. We were speechless.

The bedsit we leased in Oxford, named Folly Bridge Studio, sat right beside an 1849 building called Folly House, a perfect example of an architectural style with expensive ornamental flourishes that serve no practical purpose. And this folly was situated on the 1826 reconstruction site of an historic 1485 Folly Bridge that spanned the River Thames, which thankfully did not collapse during our stay. For the record, I don't believe in folly. It serves no constructive purpose. But for some reason folly believes in me.

The queen's death was a big deal in the UK. Ending seven decades as the longest-reigning British monarch, her legacy stands and, I can report, she was deeply loved by her people based on the outpouring of tributes we saw and the crowds of mourners and well-wishers that gathered, even in the streets of Oxford, for ceremonies on the days following her death.

Succeeded by her eldest son in a very old British game of thrones, Charles already holds his own record: at the age of seventy-three, he is the oldest ascending British monarch in the country's history.

I never had a chance to meet the queen, but my birth and Elizabeth II's official coronation both took place in 1953. Pam and I considered traveling to London to participate in the queen's state funeral but standing in the street beside the hundreds of thousands of well-wishers, throwing flowers and cheering and clapping would have felt not only chaotic but impersonal. She didn't attend my baptism and we didn't attend her funeral.

We did however celebrate the queen's life by accepting a lunch invitation from an elegant British landlady who had graciously offered to hold a £200 lodging deposit we'd made until we were able to cross the pond and pick it up. She'd received our money before COVID prevented our travel. Lodging in her home was unfortunately not available when we finally could travel in 2022.

She is a beautiful lady, and at the age of eighty-six she still inspiringly acts as the portal guardian where travelers passing to or through Oxford may stay or leave, all by the appointment of Irene. When we arrived for our lunch date and were invited to sit on her couch, we talked and laughed for half an hour while her personally prepared lunch finished baking and we felt luxuriously welcomed. Sitting in an upholstered chair across from us, buttoned in her cardigan vest and surrounded by her photos—the faces of so many loved members of her family we'd never met—she demonstrated how resplendently simple hospitality could be.

Ten years younger than the queen, she had graciously stepped in to welcome us. Somebody had to. This was England after all. A glass of wine? A cup of tea? Then salmon, new potatoes, asparagus and cherry tomatoes bright as the Crown Jewels, with an apple crumble for dessert, topped by a dollop of rich whipped cream. How like Elizabeth, how sweet, this audience with Irene.

Eventually we said our goodbyes at the door, thanking this reigning hostess for inviting us to her home. It proved to be important, a memorable part of our trip that satisfied our appetite for adventure. On the walk across Oxford, back to the room we ultimately leased, we speculated about our canceled holiday—the one we had missed—how our original plans could have been irreparably lost. Of course, most of our visit hadn't been affected, like touring the museums, hiking along the ancient Thames, taking pictures of buildings where the architecture revealed an antiquity we rarely see in America. We boarded trains that took us to Stratford-on-Avon and Bath, stared into the heavens of stained-glass cathedrals, stood silently beside the graves of literary heroes, like Tolkien, C.S. Lewis, and Agatha Christie.

We did most of the things we likely would have done had we arrived in 2021, and except for that one royal revision that tripped up the entire country while they mourned their loss and celebrated the life of their longest-reigning monarch, we might have never understood how the ending of a life can reveal the character of a living nation.

PASSPORTS, PLEASE!

As I reached into my desk drawer to retrieve my recently expired passport, a version of my 1970's self emerged. Before me was a young man I hardly recognized. He had hair down to his shoulders, a poor excuse for a beard, and a silly look on his face. My mother-in-law used to declare he looked just like Jesus, as if she'd formally met the man.

Eventually I found the correct expired passport, then gasped again. This codger staring back at me looked too much like a short-timer, closer than I realized to crossing into that territory where return trips are strictly prohibited.

I've held three official U.S. passports, the first one issued in 1979, the second in 1995, and the third one in 2008. They permitted me to travel internationally six times. With these expired documents languishing in my desk drawer, I faced a dilemma. Should I renew?

Renewal is such a tricky word. While it implies a kind of rebirth, it also contains the dregs of fiscal responsibility, like renewing vehicle registration, coughing up more cash for insurance premiums, or deciding which magazine subscriptions might get more use in an office waiting room.

Our government collects $145 from first-time applicants, and a mere $110 for renewal, as long as the citizen's previous passport was issued in the last fifteen years. An acceptable photograph is also required, a head shot that most post offices can furnish for an additional $15, even if there's a chance your face will eventually show up under a stamp.

I'd have tried to submit my own photo but government regulations are very specific. Any variation from the more than twenty-three mandates covering size, resolution, pose, expression, background, attire, or even the accurate depiction of skin tone can result in rejection. Upon studying the rules, I wondered about the training passport personnel receive to decide if one's skin tone is accurate and consequently acceptable. Politics these days still prompt questions like these. Once issued, a passport is a valid for exactly ten years.

With my mostly miserly midwestern ways, I figured I had no option but to renew. Despite being gifted with second-rate math skills, I calculated that ten years of inflation multiplied by the largest national debt in the world divided by my actuarial risks of survival would add up to saving a few dollars if I could ever afford to travel again.

Only one in five Americans retains a passport, preferring interstate to international travel. By letting my passport lapse, I'd be joining the majority of Americans who for one reason or another prefer to stay at home. Granted, the U.S. is huge, with plenty of opportunities for domestic tourism, but as Shakespeare might have phrased it, "All the world's a stage . . . except America, which has remodeled itself into a movie theater."

Six trips abroad and I felt welcome in every port, airport, or station by the people who worked and lived there. In Paris I almost took the wrong train to the Palace of Versailles, the one traveling away from it instead of toward it. Through the combined efforts of a little elderly Parisian lady who spoke no English and a German tourist who spoke just a little, we managed to reorient my disorientation.

In Malta, a bus driver delayed his departure after shouting at a few impatient passengers to explain how his bus was an individual part of a fleet of vintage buses, all of them owned by locals who spent their own money customizing and decorating them. They qualified as mechanical works of art. I spent the next week trying out various bus routes just to see how creative the Maltese owners could be. Modernization has since reduced the colorful island's buses to a nondescript example of any city's strictly reliable and functional transport. Que será, será. You'd have to have been there to see it.

When friends narrate the horror stories from their travels, I nod my head and try to appear sympathetic, but safety and good luck are not simply products of staying at home. If they were, nobody would ever leave. Something about travel, especially to places you could not have imagined, opens itself to all kinds of pleasures, like sampling new foods, trying to out-grimace a gargoyle, spending money that looks phony as Monopoly cash, or stopping to stare at an architectural masterpiece still standing like a time machine after five centuries, and then getting the chance to step inside.

My new passport photo turned out to be a little glossy just above the forehead, where hair is supposed to grow, so the postal employee readjusted the lighting and took an alternative. He showed me the result and declared it should be acceptable. As a mug shot, I couldn't complain, but privately I still think it displayed more skin up there than necessary.

ROAD WORRIERS

A long holiday weekend only encourages me to stay home. No sense planning a road trip at the risk of being maimed or even killed in an accident. Self-preservation, that's the key to a long life, and nobody knows this better than retired folks. Give all the non-retired vacationers all the time they need to get back to work or school or whatever life of crime sustains the family, and that's when I start unfolding my maps.

As a child, I sat in the backseat of my parents' car, my eyes glued to the window until the motion of the vehicle rocked me to sleep. In college, my thumb managed to get me down the road. Once I could afford my own reliable transportation I didn't hang around home. I drove, sometimes like a maniac, and I didn't even buckle my seat belt or pack spare underwear. During my career years, my employers organized my expeditions into those traditional slots known as vacations. Like a rubber band, I was tethered by how far I could stretch my days off, and the whiplash from getting back on time took its toll.

Now the day I leave is flexible and the day I return is negotiable. That's not exactly a definition of freedom, but it's as close to a vagabond as I care to get.

Recently I was forced to rent a vehicle for ten days while my only transportation was in the shop. The agent on the business side of the rental desk asked if I was under seventy. I started to worry whether he really needed to know? Apparently he did, because more car rental agencies, even major ones like Avis or Hertz, are imposing maximum age limits for drivers, not just minimum. Although there is no standard policy in this country, some European, African, and South Pacific nations already impose a seventy or seventy-five age restriction, And a few U.S. carriers are setting their cruise control at the same limit. In a few years, it might not be easy for me to get out of town.

One more worry that surfaces when I start planning a road trip involves where I'll sleep. It's not that I'm unreasonably finicky about accommodations, but rest area picnic tables and a reclined bucket seat have lost their appeal. Motels are always a crapshoot when it comes to finding cleanliness and comfort on the fly. Nobody wants to say it, but the chances of coming upon a good motel for under a hundred bucks is like walking into a public toilet and discovering a clean and comfortable seat.

I need to start packing for a road trip at least five days before I leave because it gives me enough time to remember the items I'm likely to forget, for unpacking and repacking the same items in two or three alternate configurations, for removing the stuff I finally decide I'll never use, and then reassuring myself I'll have sufficient time to put it back again after I've processed the nightmares of being stranded in a foreign country jail without, say, my favorite spare belt.

What I'm going to eat can constipate my thinking when I'm planning a trip. It's not impossible to pack healthy food in ice chests and stay away from the fast-food feeding troughs, but I don't want to. What fun is being on the road, freewheeling, when I have to be a dietary monument to responsible decision-making? Good eating choices. Vegan of the vehicle. Organic overdrive.

I work hard to choose a sensible diet when I'm at home. On the road, I'm with Jack Kerouac: "I ate another apple pie and ice cream; that's practically all I ate all the way across the country, I knew it was nutritious and it was delicious." My road trips will never inspire a generation, which is why it's necessary that they at least inspire me.

I returned from my ten-day trip to Devils Tower in just seven days. I may have been worried about things back home, or maybe the thought of operating someone else's car without the desire to drive like Mad Max took the exhaust out of my sails. But I saw no aliens, although everyone I talked to warned me about the possibility. I learned there are parts of Wyoming where driving at or above eighty miles an hour is not such a bad idea. I learned that the rabbit population of Wyoming might be on the brink of extinction based on the number of squashed bunnies that littered the highways. I also learned that people who live in Wyoming are collectively called Wyomingites, which is better than being mistaken for a Nutmegger if you drive through Connecticut. I worry about that.

2: INSTEAD OF YOUR NEIGHBORS

ACCESS DENIED

I patiently waited for the man in front of me to explain why the overdue DVD he checked out from the library could not have been checked out by him. He suggested to the librarian she had made a mistake, then quickly—after noticing the daggers in her glance—asked, rather rhetorically, if maybe someone might have used his library card without his knowledge.

"It happens," was all she said, then she double-checked some additional library records and concluded that, yes, the item was still missing. The man went away muttering the most ingenious combination of curses and apologies I'd ever heard.

When it was my turn, I stated my business. "May I please have your internet password?"

She looked at me as if I'd arrived from a different planet. "We don't give out our password."

"You mean the public isn't allowed access to the internet at this library?"

"I didn't say that. You will have to hand your device to me and I will input the password."

I'd never visited a library where this level of internet security served as the protocol. Edward Snowdon would have been stymied had NSA headquarters followed the Bisbee Public Library model for thwarting troublemakers. I had no choice, so I passed my device across the desk. She tipped my iPad screen up so I couldn't peek, then digitized my access with six strokes of a very nimble digit of her own. She gave me a final silent facial recognition scan before returning my property, as if trying to assess the kind of threat I might pose.

My mistake. I asked for a password. Patrons of this library obviously know enough not to ask. Or, more than likely, I was just being paranoid.

Password security is always big news in this cyber age, especially when a fresh batch of corporate customer records has been hacked. Who cares if our government spies on its own citizens? At least the White House isn't involved in an Amazon spending spree using our credit card information.

A review of last year's top passwords revealed the popularity of these three choices: 123456, the word "password," and 12345678. Online users that pick these wispy strings of characters to foil hackers are considered "beyond help" by security experts but handing your hardware to a complete stranger in order to access the internet doesn't seem all that sophisticated either.

For five years, I worked in the technical services department of an old Carnegie library back in the 1970s, when anyone's use of the phrase "the net" might involve a fishing story about landing a big walleye. I typed all the necessary cataloging information using an IBM Selectric on recipe-sized cards and pockets that I pasted inside each new book so our materials could pass securely through the checkout line. Back then, a "barcode" still referred to a quick way to order a drink. Audio CDs were just becoming a snazzy new media available for the price of a library card. Passwords were not a part of our library's jargon. The best way to keep the unwashed public out was to lock the doors and hide the key. Near the end of the decade the new director hired a new boss for my department, a genius in technology, who gently nudged his employees toward the lexicon of the digital age.

It may be, despite nearly forty years of sophistication and progress, that the public still has a lock-and-key mentality when it comes to internet security. We reuse the same old passwords at multiple sites, think our pet names could riddle a Gollum, and we balk at devising better data codes because it's too difficult to remember our momentary inspiration.

I should know. I created a document that is three pages long with all my usernames and passwords, a feat I thought awfully clever until my retired friend and ex-department boss explained how easily such a document could be stolen. My cyber-life would become an open book. He showed me how to encrypt access to my cyber-biography, but recently I've forgotten the password that allows me access to my own cache of passwords.

My newest strategy (which I'm still theoretically testing) involves tattooing a single personal password in a very sensitive location on my body. The experts warn us that no method can ever be foolproof, and I'll probably feel like a fool checking every time I forget my password, but at least I'm confident that not too many complete strangers will ask to handle my device, nor will I be asking to handle theirs.

A THING LEARNED

Some of us hope the lessons we've learned as young people serve us as we grow older, and that the lessons we impart as adults play an important role in the development of younger lives. As for breaking the law, that can happen at any age.

After the officer wrote the speeding ticket, he passed it through the pickup's open window to an aged but all-too-familiar hand, an arthritic one that belonged to a former public-school employee, a retired man who'd worked the disciplinary beat at the same junior high school where the officer once attended classes as a boy.

The two knew each other well, perhaps too well, because the boy had been sent to the front office on more than one occasion to receive a disciplinarian's paddling. The vice-principal's job back then was to intervene, and he was trained to respond when misbehavior arose. His technique required the child to bend over his desk, then to deliver one firm whack, before stopping to ask, "Is one enough?"

For most students, one swat was more than enough, but some of the incorrigibles refused to give in and the paddle for this particular child's behind had landed repeatedly until it was the adult who finally had to give in, which speaks volumes for the tenacity of some youth.

As the retired school official reached to accept his speeding ticket, the officer held it tighter, just for a second. "Is one enough?" the young officer asked. The old man nodded, "Yes sir, one is more than enough." The officer smiled and returned to his patrol car. The moment had come to him like a charm. He would remember writing this citation for the rest of his life.

His career in law enforcement, however, did not endure like that of his high school disciplinarian. The young police officer married and found new employment in the business world, a job where he could afford to raise his own children. As a father, he'd also have occasion to develop his own style of discipline. Any dedicated parent must deal with the trouble when children learn to test their willpower against the house rules. A spanking has served as a template for many parents, and some spirited children can attest to the expediency of this model only as they mature.

It was the ex-student-ex-officer-turned-business-man who shared the speeding ticket story with me, not the retired disciplinarian. I had been the young man's high school English teacher. We crossed paths again much later in life, completely by chance, while I was shopping for a vehicle. He sold me a used car, and more—he told me this story, which I have carried with me for more than a decade.

I also knew the retired disciplinarian, met him when I first moved to the area in the early 1980s. He always impressed me as a kind and generous, hard-working, good-old-boy kind of guy who "yes ma'amed" my wife for the thirty years we were acquainted. Even more curious, he made a habit of launching a friendly wave to nearly every driver that passed by, because he knew much of the population in our little town. Educators are like that. They carry their encounters their entire lives, like scrapbooks that constantly need updating.

Eventually people age, people die. Everyone who knew the old man in our little town was shocked and saddened. We thought that just like his old brown pickup—one he'd purchased new in 1971—he would keep on running, up and down our county roads forever. Apparently life doesn't get that kind of mileage.

I had the chance to tell my old friend before he died about my encounter with his former behavior-challenged student. He remembered every detail of the incident, nodding at each unfolding of the plot as I retold the speeding-ticket story I'd heard.

"So, if you hadn't paddled that boy's butt until it glowed, do you think he'd have let you off with just a warning?" I searched his face for any clue that he harbored some kind of resentment for the way the arresting officer treated him.

"Nope," he replied, "I don't think I had a chance and really, I deserved that ticket, because I've probably gotten away without being stopped more times than I care to count."

"But didn't you think the police officer was out of line when he threw those words back in your face?"

"Not at all. I was just proud he remembered his lesson."

ADJECTIVE DEFICIT
DISORDER

In my neighborhood, a house has been boarded up, its grass crispy and uncut, a stubble of weeds longer than a five o'clock shadow. The absent owner leaned an enormous piece of plywood against the side of the house and crudely spray-painted the words, "Trespassers Will Be Prose."

A slow walker will notice a faint attempt at including the letter C after the word Prose but for some reason the fullness of the threat never materialized. I smile whenever I walk by, because in my imagination I have already scaled the chain-link fence and responded with my own spray-painted reply, "Visitors Will Be Poetry."

As a former English teacher, I learned to tell when my students had a grasp on the most basic grammar by noticing which ones laughed when I posed this simple riddle in class: what's the difference between a cat and a comma? Of course, nobody would be laughing yet, not until I answered the riddle: one has its claws at the end of its paws, and the other is a pause at the end of a clause. At its root grammar is a kind of logic you don't have to memorize.

But everyone stumbles over language's peculiarities, and no one needs to feel guilty about being exposed with his or her modifiers dangling. Nobody's perfect, and nobody should seek that distinction. Once, I asked a doctor before undergoing a medical procedure if a colonoscopy would interfere with my ability to punctuate correctly. He scratched his head, gave me a quizzical look, and immediately put me under. I swear I heard a round of applause in the background before I lost consciousness. The abandoned house I mentioned is on display for public comment, but an internet search yields many better examples of language deficits. Lynne Truss, author of the 2003 best-selling book *Eats, Shoots & Leaves*, writes about a group I'll call "The Grammar Police" that roams streets in England, equipped with black markers and white paint, prepared to correct the most egregious errors it finds displayed. Misplaced or missing apostrophes, commas gone comatose, crippled contractions, all misspoken signage that is helpless to correct itself.

Misspellings are the most common errors, some of them simply typos, and many of them switched by a software's auto-correction feature. Occasionally a truly poetic misspelling unintentionally occurs. I've seen Thursday appear as Turdsday, which seems to me to be a perfect descriptor for having to spend one more day at work so close to the thought of Friday.

These mistakes riddel many of the documents we reed too quickly without taking enough time to proofread.

I tried to explain to an ex-student's mother why it's important to be aware of errors, without trying to get past, present, or even future tense about it.

"My son has no idea what an adjective is."

"That's not unusual for a ninth grader."

"But he doesn't want to know."

"That's not so strange either. Most adults hate grammar."

"How will he ever be able to describe what's going on inside of him?"

"Adjectives aren't the only parts of speech that describe."

"I have a confession."

"I know, you're not sure what an adjective is either."

"It's a genetic flaw. Not even my parents had a clue."

"Relax. Millions of people lead full and happy lives without knowing."

"Do you think if I study up and start using them my son will get interested?"

"You've already been using them."

"I'm sorry, I wasn't paying attention."

"No apology necessary."

"Apology. That's an adjective, isn't it?"

"No, apology is a noun, but sorry is an adjective."

"How can sorry be an adjective when it's an apology?"

"The labyrinths of grammar are complicated."

"What's a labyrinths?"

"Labyrinth is a noun, labyrinths is the plural form of the noun."

"I feel so stupid."

"Stupid is an adjective."

"Oh, well then, I feel so adjective."

"Actually, the word 'adjective' is a noun."

"Is there a pill I can take to help me?"

"Grammar itself is a pill."

"I swear I took it, but I never passed it."

"It takes a lifetime to digest."

NO OUTLET

W hen we arrived in Tucson, dragging our little thirteen-foot Scamp trailer behind us, I was reminded of W.C. Fields who'd coined a memorable phrase describing how he dragged his canoe behind him while carving his way through a wall of human flesh. Luckily, we only had to carve our way through Tucson's rush-hour traffic.

Using a dog-eared atlas, Pam plotted the path of least resistance through the northern suburbs on our way to Mount Lemmon. I can't remember ever running my truck air-conditioner in late February, but the temperature outside hovered near ninety and the engine was working hard, hauling our load. Our friends promised it would be cooler in the mountains. And quieter.

We'd never camped above Tucson, among the saguaros. We hoped they would tickle us with their prickly shade. Molino Basin, a Forest Service facility, is supposedly crowded only on the weekends and the campground does not accept reservations, so we hoped the rumor was true. If not, we'd driven ten hard hours on a lark. Plus our backup plan was lame: find a motel and leave our trailer locked up in the parking lot. But at this point it all amounted to speculation. First we'd have to find our way up the mountain.

"Stay on East Ina, then Skyline to Sunrise, then it looks like North Kolb, which should put us on Sabino Canyon Road," my GPS instructed. She's an organic navigational system—the woman in the seat beside me—so I used the option of asking questions.

"How soon before the first turn?"

"No turns what-so-ever. By the looks of this map, Ina becomes Skyline and Skyline transforms itself into Sunrise and Kolb. It's all one road."

"Then why do they keep changing its name?"

"Boredom?" was all the reply I heard before an SUV honked and sped around us, one finger signaling its intention. We encountered many more traffic maneuvers like this before we made it to the safety of our campground.

We also discovered a few more subtle insights about Tucson road planning, the most important being that no city I've ever driven through posts as many side roads with "No Outlet" signs (roughly translated: dead ends), making what I'm calling "the Tucson turn" not just fashionable, but indispensable.

Take Snyder Road, for example. To reach Catalina Highway from the north side of town, a driver is required to make an elaborate detour, adding many miles to a potentially simple route, had the crow been allowed to choose.

Naively, the GPS got excited and announced, "The next road goes in the direction we want to go," and I flicked on my left turn signal and exited Sabino Canyon.

At first Snyder looked promising. It manifested itself like a golden shortcut, eliminating any possibility of merging onto Tanque Verde, or Wrightstown or Bear Canyon, which would inevitably lead to unscheduled U-turns after missing the intersections I needed. The sun had nearly gone down and my butt complained about its seat time. Oh please, I silently wished, let Snyder be my Northwest Passage.

It wasn't. What's worse, the road itself was sweet. It meandered through a lovely neighborhood of houses, and it remained virtually free of traffic signals. If it took us to Catalina Highway I would stop the truck, get out, and kiss the desert sand. Instead, it petered out, emptied into an arroyo without so much as announcing its intention to do so. It ended. Stopped. Was no more.

We both stepped out of the truck and stared in disbe-lief. Then I backed up, and we retraced our route back toward the busy side of town.

Eventually we negotiated the traffic and found Catalina Highway, only to pass what appeared to be the other half of Snyder Road.

"I'm sorry," I sputtered, "but I've got to take this left just to see where and *if* we missed a turn." And I executed another U-turn.

When the pavement ended we were on the other side of the same arroyo where we'd been foiled half an hour ago. We climbed out of the truck and stared across the divide, the ghosts of our optimism staring back at us.

"Come on," I said. "let's get out of here before we find ourselves stuck in some kind of vortex."

I fired up the engine and executed my final Tucson turn, 180 degrees of Deja vu, and the GPS just laughed.

THE DRAIN GAME

When I first learned that the gullies along most county roads in the American Southwest are referred to as bar ditches, I thought they were named for the unfortunate drivers who'd consumed a few too many drinks before heading home and ended up in them. Although I was wrong, ample circumstantial evidence exists to make a case for updating the etymology on the subject.

It seems a bar ditch, also referred to as a barrow pit, is just a channel excavated for drainage purposes. In my neighborhood, irrigation and runoff water sluices through the cattails and the willows, creating a lush and muddy mess along the way, all of it a wetland wonderland, as long as a person can avoid climbing into one to unclog a county culvert.

Before I get around to complaining about my bar ditch, it's only proper that I take a moment to extol the virtues of the entire rural, Southwestern drainage system. It has, after all, been entrenched in the county's memory for a long, long time.

Habitat is a perk for creatures living near one. Nothing is so picturesque as a gallery of redwing blackbirds perched on the cattails, supervising traffic while overseeing the future of their young. Foxes, skunks, pheasants, feral kittens and cats, dogs, raccoons, and the occasional pair of ducks all make use of the dense growth prompted by a continuous supply of water to sustain and shelter their wild rural lives.

A bar ditch is also a blessing in the spring when the asparagus rises. Vehicles pull to the side of the road and someone in rubber boots or ragged tennis shoes wielding a sharp knife swiftly collects the tender shoots. Some of these asparagus beds have been producing so regularly and prolifically over the decades that other people would like to keep these locations for themselves. A distant gunshot or a crescendo of barking dogs is usually reason enough to consider relocating down the road.

Then there are the plumes of dust that drivers spew, often while traveling twenty miles per hour over the posted speed limit, gravel spitting from their tires like nails from a pneumatic gun. Add a stiff wind from the prevailing direction and it's possible to relive the Dust

Bowl era if you own a house beside a county road. Add to that recipe the mud that will coat your vehicle's lower panels all the way up to the door handles when it rains, and you have a fairly obvious transition to the part about me complaining.

My house is in a peculiar position, given the natural rise and fall of the land. If I were to compare my property to a bathtub, my driveway would start about where the drain is located. A twelve-inch culvert, probably installed while all of today's county commissioners were either attending or complaining about Woodstock, channels the runoff from the bar ditch under the road to its opposite side. That's the plan, and for most of the year it kinda works.

When it doesn't, like during a spring, summer, or autumn downpour, a sheet of water rolls across my neighbor's property and creates a lake where my yard used to be. I am happy to report that since I've lived here the water has never washed out the county road, which is what a bar ditch is supposed to prevent, but once a year a drainage flood backs up toward my house, washes a channel of gravel out my driveway, spills over its grade, and turns my septic field into a wading pool. That's when you'll find me standing ankle deep in a brown sea, praying that my shovel might behave like a biblical staff.

The county has kindly scraped my bar ditch free of all its habitat so the water will flow better. Eventually it might install a shiny new, larger capacity culvert, one that will help handle the flow at these infrequent but peak runoff periods. What the county can't do, of course, is move massive quantities of dirt until my house is situated on an engineered plateau, so it overlooks my driveway from a vantage that gives me enough perspective to understand why any sane person would have located the house here in the first place.

Speaking of perspective, now that the gully has been scraped clean—temporarily eliminating the cattails, the willow, the asparagus, and the weeds—I am suddenly able to notice every beer can or whiskey bottle that gets tossed from the window of a moving vehicle, and I'm beginning to reassess my initial interpretation about why it's called a bar ditch.

NO WELL

A couple from rural Montezuma County, Colorado, decided on a Christmas trip to an ancient site known as the Montezuma Well, over three hundred miles away in Arizona. The drive across the Navajo reservation unfolded beautifully and uneventfully until a serious accident with fatalities along Highway 160 near Red Lake blocked traffic in all directions.

The snarl threatened to consume half the day, and to highlight the feeling of helplessness while trying to remain in a Christmas spirit, the woman started singing a chorus of "Oh well, no well, oh well, no well...." The driver glanced Scrooge-ishly in her direction, which is when a Navajo man tapped on their driver's side window.

Eventually I'll have to admit to being the driver, so let me say right now that the experience made me feel like a character in someone else's Christmas story.

It was the second time the same Navajo man had stopped to offer a curt Native editorial about the impasse. The first time, on his way to talk with a Navajo grandmother in the car behind me, he simply said, "Go around," and he pointed vaguely to the north. The second time after returning from, presumably, the scene of the accident, he urged me more adamantly and with greater detail, "Go to the wash, then go around."

Upon returning to his truck, the Navajo man fired up his engine, did a U-turn, and sped off in the direction from which we had come. Pam and I glanced at each other for a fraction of a second to consider how stupid it would be to follow him, then we followed him.

At the bottom of the hill we left the pavement, along a sandy track that paralleled a dry wash. Initially I felt relieved, remembering the mention of a wash in his last set of directions. His truck veered suddenly to the right and headed up a steep incline, careening as if a madman was at the wheel, or maybe a shaman on an angry quest. If it hadn't been for his invitation to follow, I would have sworn he was trying to shake us loose. I put my truck into four-wheel drive and stepped on the gas.

Here, I should pause to mention that the truck I was driving had been a recent purchase. I'd checked to see if the four-wheel drive worked when I bought it, but I hadn't been faced with an opportunity to really test it. I couldn't help feeling a bit excited about the way off-road things were developing. I even glanced at Pam, strapped in beside me, who'd stopped singing her makeshift Christmas carol and was smiling.

Every trip I've ever taken across the checkerboard reservation has been on pavement. Well, once when I had to pee badly, I pulled to the shoulder and scrambled down a bank toward a screen of sage, but that had been my only off-road excursion. Yet this wispy maze of dirt tracks our shaman sped along served an entire community, paths that must be wired like synapses into their brains. After the first five minutes, I had no idea which direction was north. We had to trust our guide.

At one point I thought I'd lost him and would have to find my way back to the wash and the snarl of traffic on my own. Then we came around a great dune of dirt and saw the Navajo truck parked beside another pickup, two drivers talking to each other through open windows. We stopped a respectable distance away and waited.

I know for a fact that a wave of tension surged through my brain, a fear of not belonging, combined with a giddy rush of excitement, its polar opposite. Eventually the two trucks started their engines and headed off, climbing another dune. Lucky for us, the newest truck positioned between ours and the lead one drove a bit slower. Our faith in the journey had been restored.

Zig-zagging through the red dust, feeling a little like we were touring the planet Mars, we started to relax again as this expanded caravan of three men and one woman—only two of them wise—sought a route around the unseen scene of the accident.

Half an hour later, our tires touched pavement again, and looking to the left we could see in the distance an impatient knot of vehicles still waiting to be untangled. To the right, the road to Tuba City, straight and clear.

As for the Montezuma Well, a fifteen-million gallon watermark on the parchment of the Arizona desert, we finally got there, and it was rather magnificent, but in a quiet sort of way. The desert we'd just crossed contained so many more mysteries, and I had a thirst that water doesn't even begin to quench.

OVERDUE AT THE LIBRARY

I packed the boxes tight, didn't want anything getting crushed. The donations weren't going to a soup kitchen, although their shelf life would be ten times that of any standard food stocks. These were staples to nourish the mind: books I'd gathered over the years and had finally decided to pass along. I hoped a few of them might be suitable for my local library's collection. They were all in good condition, clean and intellectually consuming.

It should come as no surprise that public libraries are forced to sell many donated books just to pay for the services they provide. They are not often the financial beneficiaries of huge endowments or government bailouts. The books that patrons donate are sorted by personnel and those that can't be used on the shelves are offered to the public in the library's revolving book sale—carts of donated material either sold annually or year-round, by the pound, the best used book bargains in town.

Half a lifetime ago I worked at a public library. I'd landed the job after graduating from college with an English major, but literature was not my saving grace; rather, I could type. Not fast, but accurately. I remember being nervous at the skills test after my initial interview. I'd never even enrolled in a typing class. I couldn't type without watching my fingers on the keyboard. All my competitors finished well before my final keystroke, but the committee hired me anyway. Accuracy became my stroke of luck.

The library, a Carnegie, existed for half a century in a beautiful brown brick building with a circular staircase that took me to my desk in the upper level, overlooking the city. I loved that old place, the woodwork and history secured between those wise walls. For years, I dutifully typed my card catalog index cards, book pockets, and spine labels, thinking I could be happy growing musty and elderly in this job. Then our systems were updated: a bond issue passed to build a larger, more modern library. My wooden desk was replaced with a padded cubicle in the new building's basement, officially referred to as "the lower level." The Carnegie was demolished. I lasted two more years before completing a teaching certification, then traded the comfort of books for the screech of chalk on a chalkboard.

Personally I have no regrets, but still loved the dignity of such a revered institution, the public library, until the donations librarian explained the disheveled character of this once grand establishment. Our libraries, she said, have turned into bus stations. At first, I hoped she was employing a clever metaphor about the power of books, able to transport readers to distant places. But no, she felt she'd been presiding over the mayhem as our libraries disintegrate into hangouts for drifters, shelters for hangover recovery. Vomit in the restrooms. Vandalism in shadowy corners. The refusal to obey rules and outright theft. Belligerence at the checkout desk. The hush I always appreciated falling like a velvet curtain as each person passed through the front doors is being replaced by a hubbub of self-indulgence.

Here's an illustrated explanation: a woman sitting quietly near our library's window that faces the park is reading a magazine. She thinks she hears the pitter-patter of raindrops. She glances up but the sun is shining, so she looks to where the sound seems to come from and sees a man peeing on the metal shelving. The desk librarian ends up chasing him outside, all this going on while he grabs himself and tries to zip up, shouting, "It wasn't me." But of course, it was.

Larger libraries across the country have a developing strategy to deal with their behaviorally challenged patrons by introducing social workers into their staffing—personnel with the training to deal with the kind of people who show up when the doors open and go away only at the time the doors close. Some of these souls need the services a county can provide, counseling for drugs and alcohol, housing, food, medication and psychiatric care, not reference assistance. Perhaps the time has come to recognize that our libraries have a complicated mission, one that has changed over time. To expect personnel trained in research and book cataloging as well as information dissemination to confront these problems is not only unfair but dangerous to everyone involved.

These things called books, two boxes of them in my backseat, are tokens of a radical idea, that knowledge and the imagination do not belong to the privileged few. But that bus is leaving the station. Perhaps it's time we get onboard, not just stand in the parking lot and wave goodbye.

CARS IN OUR STARS

I t requires determination to reach the Nebraska pan-
handle, an area wedged between South Dakota,
Wyoming, and the northeast corner of Colorado. Some
might go so far as to say there's little to recommend the
attempt. But over 60,000 visitors set their sights on a
strange tourist site every year, what has been dubbed
"one of our nation's ten wackiest attractions." After
decades of promises to myself, I finally managed an
up-close encounter, between its official dedication on
the summer solstice of 1987 and its enormous gathering
that camped out for a glimpse of 2017's once-in-a-life-
time total solar eclipse.

Carhenge depicts a recycled piece of history, an
impulsively accurate replica of England's prehistoric
Stonehenge ruins which have been falling apart on the
Salisbury plain since 2000 BC. Like its ancient coun-
terpart, Carhenge occupies a circle containing three
standing vehicle-trilithons, two station car-stones, an

automobile-heel stone, and a clunker-slaughter stone, all placed to mimic the original.

As its updated name suggests, nobody dragged monolithic stones across the Nebraska Sandhills to engineer the Carhenge installation. In 1987, artist Jim Reinders retrieved thirty-nine dilapidated heaps from local sources, mid-twentieth century American auto salvage, pumped up the tires and rolled them into the circle, completing the work in six days. Twenty-two cars tipped into five-foot trenches stand with their headlights pointing toward the stars. Eight are laid flat and welded across upright car pillars to imitate traditional trilithon arches. Eventually painted grey, the entire structure mimics the color of stone, although I suspect the family just wanted to avoid the unavoidable chore of washing and waxing the cars.

Carhenge is not a tribute to classic American automobiles, although any savvy autophile might easily identify a '61 Cadillac DeVille, a '65 Chevelle, and a '51 Willys Jeep in the mix. Overall, the cars lack luster. They qualify as carcasses rescued from the jaws of the crusher. The monument originated as a tribute to the artist's father, but the finished product also qualifies as an elaborate tribute to parody.

A 2017 interview with ninety-year-old Jim Reinders is available on YouTube. You can still see the twinkle in his eye as he recounts his personal history working for an international oil company as a petroleum engineer, being shifted to many locations around the globe. His stay in London—his favorite assignment—provided plenty of up-close time with Carhenge's distant relative, a place he loved to visit and revisit while living in the UK.

Standing in the Carhenge parking lot, glancing across its ten-acre field, I could appreciate how perfectly the Reinders clan memorialized America. After all, most people arrive at this remote site north of Alliance, Nebraska by car—our legacy to the world—like it or not.

Erecting the monument required a family crew of about thirty-five relatives and friends. Of that monumental undertaking, the artist writes: "We were able to reduce the time of the original Stonehenge construction by 9,999 years and fifty-one weeks." And as if to drive the point of America's automotive birthright home, three small foreign cars are buried on the Carhenge site with this sign: "Here lie three bones of foreign cars . . . they served our purpose while Detroit slept." A wisecrack delivered by a high priest of irony.

The sculpture received much criticism when first completed. Detractors maintained it was an eyesore and should be torn down. I wish this sort of sentiment would erupt in my neighborhood where salvage litters the landscape of backyards and backlots. I even know of one place where a buried car with its windows rolled up served as a makeshift septic tank.

A group known as the Friends of Carhenge rescued the monument. While grumpy neighbors complained, loosely organized defenders claimed the installation had enough market potential to enhance the local economy. Political bickering ensued. Eventually a comment box appeared on site where visitors reacted to what they'd seen, and an overwhelming unspoken support for the project emerged, not only among the community, but also among a small but growing tourist population. Eventually Reinders gave the ten acres to the city of Alliance and one of the "wackiest attractions" in America found a semi-permanent place on the map.

I say "semi-permanent" because in the earthly game of rock, metal, and scissors Stonehenge will outlast Carhenge. But if visitor statistics continue to surge, it's only a matter of time before the city council proposes sacrificing the occasional city council member as an additional tourist attraction.

FLEDGLING FLAGS

While out for a brisk walk—also known as my morning constitutional—I paused across from a flag that hung beside a neighborhood front door. It resembled an American flag, but this one fluttered grey, as if it had been rolled in a scuttle of cold ashes. I rubbed my eyes, thinking I'd suddenly gone colorblind, then noticed a single bright blue stripe on the field of grey. I scratched my head, convinced an appointment with an optometrist was long overdue.

Returning home, however, I decided to search the internet for an answer and found that a fleet of freshly manufactured flags has become popular. These flags, labeled "thin line flags," are available for purchase from many online sites, a product that transforms our stars and stripes into a declaration of preference instead of independence, like the blue stripe version which pledges an allegiance to the police. Other thin stripe color options vary, from green to purple, from silver to orange, and from red to yellow to black. Each color designates a separate allegiance tacked to a diminished field of what has uniformly been honored for over two hundred years as the old red, white, and blue.

Even the veracity of Betsy Ross's role in designing the first Stars & Stripes has been questioned by historians, but it cannot be denied that she did make flags for fifty years following the Revolution. We have receipts for Garrison flags for the U.S. Arsenal and ship flags for the Pennsylvania Naval Fleet, so we know the flags didn't come from China.

An apocryphal story about Betsy Ross's involvement with our first flag describes a meeting with George Washington. He showed up at her house with a sketch for a flag, seeking an upholsterer who could stitch this new nation a durable emblem for its future. His sketch offered a circular pattern of thirteen six-pointed stars, one for each of the colonies, all white and all unified on a field of blue. Ross demonstrated how it would be quicker for her to cut five-pointed stars and Washington saw the merits of her suggestion. Negotiations never flagged, and a deal was struck. America had its symbol of freedom.

Unfortunately, understanding our "thin line flags" requires the viewer to interpret a new color code. We can assume the online customer knows what his or her flag stands for when ordering it, but neighbors might scratch their heads once it gets hoisted up the pole. For those, like me, who might be a little confused, I thought a color key might help. A green line represents support for federal agents, park rangers, and the Border Patrol; a blue line identifies an allegiance to the police; a yellow line embodies support for security guards and tow-truck drivers; a silver line designates support for corrections officers; a red line signifies fire department support; a gold line denotes support for 911 operators and police dispatchers (as opposed to just the police); an orange line symbolizes support for the Search and Rescue and EMS personnel; a purple line personifies support for persons who died or suffered great injury while in political office due to violence.

See what I mean? You need a secret decoder ring to figure out what you're saluting. I've omitted a few stripes, because my dictionary is running out of synonyms for the word "represents" and not surprisingly, the manufacturers have an ample variety of colors. Even more frustrating is that a customer can combine color options on the same flag using shorter stripes crammed into a single line to express support for multiple organizations: the thin blue/red/green line, for example. So much for an American flag that once sought to unify a nation. Now, we can assemble and declare our allegiances like a jigsaw puzzle.

The thin stripe flag is really a marketing idea hoisted up the flagpole, a Go-Fund-Me event for patriotism. Since I completed my effort to figure out what each color represents, the pop-up ads keep appearing like digital flags flying all over my browser screens. Still, my search made me wonder, what color, for instance, is the stripe of support for America's teachers? I hunted for one, perhaps a chalky white stripe with a cluster of gold stars for good behavior? I couldn't find it, despite the four million Americans who have dedicated their lives to this essential public service. And what about other worthy champions, like our nation's investigative reporters or our peaceful protesters, who fail to meet the prerequisites for earning their stripes on a murky field of grey?

You see, I think the problem with these new flags is simple: some of our nation's heroes simply stand a little too far to the left of that thin line that seeks to divide us.

AN ECONOMICS PRIMER

"Money is our madness, our vast collective madness" —D.H. Lawrence

S ome financial news junkies still associate "trick-le-down economics" with Ronald Reagan, our fortieth president, who popularized a policy of tax cuts for the wealthy because, as the theory goes, the money would eventually find its way to the working class as surely as water moves from higher to lower ground. Back in 1981, just like a schoolteacher would, the President provided a big visual chart that he pointed to during a television broadcast, as if it were a chalkboard and the lesson was easy as pie.

But even before Reaganomics, presidents and pundits both endorsed or disavowed this fiscal concept, as far back as 1932 when Will Rogers coined the phrase:

"The money was all appropriated for the top in the hopes that it would trickle down to the needy. Mr. Hoover didn't know that money trickled up. Give it to the people at the bottom and the people at the top will have it before night."

Unemployed families waiting in long lines for food ought to remind us the economy isn't working for everyone. Hoarded household staples, a tangled supply chain, and our health care system overloaded to a point of breaking suggest it is time for a new economic metaphor. We are simply not enduring a sluggish trickle down. It's more like constipation, what I will refer to hereafter as an improperly functioning digestive economy—one where the money that goes in at the top just isn't coming out at the bottom.

Proper digestion is easier to understand than finances. Wikipedia explains the body's processing of food as "the breakdown of large insoluble food molecules into small water-soluble food molecules so that they can be absorbed into the watery blood plasma." Lean times demand a strength of character, but statistical fiscal formulas are hardly food for thought.

Translated into edible terms, the 2017 Tax Cuts and Jobs Act provided a grocery stockpile for the wealthy. The top one percent consumed more sirloin, lobster,

Black Forest chocolate cake, and lemon meringue pie. The rest of us managed to sneak in a slim helping of pizza, rice, hamburgers, and cookies even at the height of the good times. You see, if we consider economics biologically, groceries only nourish workers when they reach the digestive system, and if the decimal point isn't located in the right place it doesn't work.

Here's where the whole thing gets rather messy. I watched Wall Street hemorrhage gains and losses every day for a month and it made me feel queasy, like riding on a roller coaster. But investors and traders survive on a diet of fear and elation, the financial equivalent of an irritable bowel syndrome. It's a way of life for them, although for the rest of us not a healthy one. The stock market is said to function as a gauge for our economic well-being but obsessing about Wall Street won't promote regularity.

A thriving democracy requires cash flow, not speculation, whimsy, or self-congratulatory antics, and a nation certainly will not survive by depending on that loaf of highly processed and dangerously malleable white bread in the White House. You see, a strong leader nourishes the whole nation. When the electorate advances a glut of rich and fatty foods, the body politic suffers. It's time for a healthier diet.

In one form or another what goes in must eventually come out, and if it doesn't the people at the top should be the ones experiencing cramps, anxiety, and that miserable bloated feeling. They never do, although when resources are distributed fairly we all grow a little stronger. Real food provides energy, shelter bestows safety, and a genuine education imparts the insight to recognize the difference between a healthy diet and a quick snack on political convenience food.

Trickle-down shifts very little to those who need it. A modest individual tax reduction like the one passed in 2017 impersonates a cafe's daily special because it is designed to quickly expire. The corporate tax breaks, however, were significant, and they were legislated to be permanent, which means the old axiom is true: the top can have its cake and eat it, too. In order to maintain the practice of feeding the overfed, workers are expected to put more and more from their pantries back into the government cupboard.

Digestive economics has one special advantage over any other strategy. Generally, you know when you're full. Maybe if we thought of our nation's wealth as food, opening the larder and sharing the bounty would be so much more satisfying than the continual struggle to upgrade the vault's security system. Food offers a fresher metaphor. Of course, locked away or hoarded, even food spoils, which is when it should be used as fertilizer.

3: WORSHIP A DOMESTIC DEITY OR TWO

DEAR ABBIE

I should have written this book review when your book first appeared, not waited like I have until readers forgot about it, but thirty-eight years late is probably better than never.

Back in the early seventies when I worked as a public library employee, a patron submitted an interlibrary loan request for Abbie Hoffman's *Steal This Book*. I knew very little about Hoffman at the time except as a news item, for protests associated with the Vietnam War. He was, I learned, one of the Chicago Seven, tried and convicted (the conviction was later overturned) for inciting riots in Chicago during the 1968 Democratic Convention.

Dutifully, I sat down at my teletype machine and forwarded the library patron's request. I'll never forget the reply that arrived the next day: This book has been stolen from all holding libraries. I was impressed. To be able to write a book seemed magical, but to inspire legions of readers to walk off with the thing bordered on the absurd. Here was marketing gone mad, but in a way that surprised me.

I never actually read Hoffman's book, not until last month when a used bookstore copy surfaced in Flagstaff. It's actually a facsimile edition printed in 1996, nearly a decade after Abbie Hoffman killed himself by overdose. According to those who believe in conspiracies, the jury is still out on that conclusion. Strangely, what he outlines in his "Table of Discontents" is nothing short of declaring war on the system. The FBI kept a file on Hoffman's activities that amounted to 13,262 pages. That's 12,954 more pages than Hoffman's actual book! Still, as a radical and part-time underground fugitive, Hoffman inspired a generation to question authority and in every possible way rip off the system, something many people are very committed to, even today. Illegal downloads and pirated movies rank high as popular domestic abuse, while Ponzi schemes and mismanaged banking practices have made the hit list as corporate criminal misconduct. In his book, Hoffman openly advocates illegal behavior, but he always maintains "corporate feudalism [is] the only robbery worthy of being called a 'crime,' for it is committed against the people as a whole."

Hoffman's book obsesses on the idea of getting things for free by scheme or outright theft. 1970s society was shocked by what he had to say, but Hoffman only touched a nerve that pretty much functions today as a pulse. Any economic meltdown emphasizes this trend—a new kind of American Free-dumb, just another word for nothing left to steal. Hoffman's book might just as well be republished and sold, titled to appeal to today's pseudo revolutionaries: *Steal This Loan*, *Steal This Home*, *Steal This Medicare*, *Steal This Retirement Fund*, *Steal This Bonus*, or *Steal This Identity*.

At his funeral, a Rabbi eulogized Hoffman's life as an embodiment of a Jewish tradition, one that seeks to "comfort the afflicted and afflict the comfortable." To that end, Hoffman's entire book is readily available on the internet for anyone to use, for free, sponsored by sites dedicated to keeping his style of political activism alive, but if you want to pilfer the book like a true Yippie of the 70s, pull up in the dark to an unsuspecting and security-lax Wi-Fi hot spot in your neighborhood and steal his signal. It's not exactly illegal, but if you're sitting at home worrying about losing your job, a distraction might be just what you need.

EXIT LAUGHING

George Carlin, May 12, 1937-June 22, 2008

In Las Vegas, if you stare up from the Strip at all the flashing billboards announcing which eternally recycled performers will be appearing, it's easy to come to the conclusion that, sadly, there are no new talented performers alive in America. At least not in Las Vegas. I mean, there's Wayne Newton, Siegfried and a bit of Roy, Celine Dion, David Copperfield's magic act, and Cher, the performer who stands on her one name. Not only are they not new, but the billboards also announcing their appearances read like epitaphs.

I remember long ago when I noticed George Carlin was going to appear on the Strip. I wanted so badly to see his show, but the bank wouldn't loan me the money for a down payment on his tickets. I had to settle for a recording I found at a second-hand audio store. I listened to him at home and just laughed, his imagined presence filling the little room where I sat.

It's hard to believe so many years have passed since George Carlin passed. And what a strange word for dying, Carlin might have observed, to say someone has "passed" —as if a life has just accelerated out of reach. Carlin was famous for word lists, so many of them containing euphemisms, and now the man himself has been euphemized. What a way to go.

Carlin regularly discussed death. He said, "Death is caused by swallowing small amounts of saliva over a long period of time." He also said, "I'm always relieved when someone is delivering a eulogy and I realize I'm listening to it." George, you should be ecstatic, because you don't have to listen anymore. You are in that strange place where jokes go after they are told, their impact recalled but their punch lines eternally forgotten.

Perhaps becoming cynical as we age can't be helped, but to lose the humor makes us unbalanced. The news, for instance, can't help reminding us of tragedies and the dying, that the number of people sixty-five or older is expected to double in the next three decades. Anticipating that looming threshold, Carlin claimed that eventually we'd refuse to refer to ourselves as the elderly. He suggested we call ourselves the pre-dead.

I think the man just grew wiser, not older. I own a book with his signature scrawled on the title page, one of my possessions that rises above Carlin's famous quip that our possessions are "just stuff." I found it at a thrift store, a first edition copy of *When Will Jesus Bring the Pork Chops?*. Someone just tossed it out, probably because Carlin's humor offended (and still offends) some people. Noted for his social criticism, he poked many taboo subjects squarely in the eye. He had a knack for laughing black.

Seventy-one years on this planet and he still exists in countless recordings on the internet and books that are easy to find. If he has anything left to say about humor, given his currently unique perspective from the afterlife, it's still a mystery, although more than likely very funny. I'm hoping to see his afterlife performance, eventually, but I'm going to be more than a little crabby if it still costs money.

Now for Something Completely Vonnegut

Roughly two years ago, a man of genius took an awkward fall, which amounted to his last bow, as he left the stage that Shakespeare has compared to this world. On April 11, 2007, this man exited without ever saying a direct word to me. I did manage to see him perform at Fort Lewis College in Durango, Colorado back in the early 1980s and thanks to my friend Bob, I now possess a signed copy of Vonnegut's *Timequake*.

If I had my way, Kurt Vonnegut's name would show up in dictionaries of the future, not only as a reference to the deceased author of *Slaughterhouse Five* and twenty-four other literary works, but also as a synonym for telling the truth with just enough humor to make somebody listen. I know it's difficult to imagine an author's last name used as a verb, as in, "The President tried to Vonnegut the press conference, but skepticism hung in the air like cigar smoke." Isn't the use of Vonnegut's name here so much more pleasing than having to beat around, say, a George Bush?

In his final book, *A Man Without a Country*, Vonnegut mentions the name of a British general, Henry Shrapnel, who engineered a means to send metal fragments out from an exploding shell or bomb, all for the sake of killing and maiming additional victims that the blast did not knock into obscurity. Vonnegut writes, "Don't you wish you had something named after you?" What a terrible thing, to have Shrapnel's bloody name preserved in the lexicon and not Vonnegut's. At least Alfred Nobel had the audacity to obscure his notoriety as the inventor of dynamite by dedicating his fortune to the pursuit of peace. Andrew Carnegie, the steel company magnet, attracted so much wealth that near the end of his life he gave huge sums away to build Carnegie libraries in communities all across the country. He's remembered for his generosity, not his heavy-handed labor tactics.

Thomas Crapper wasn't so lucky. Thomas (in this case I prefer the informality of first names) had no vision when it came to foreseeing how posterity would remember him. Or if he did, he must have cringed at his own ingenuity until the day he died.

Vonnegut himself was no slouch at coining words. I remember his invention for achieving sufficient speed for space travel with the word "chronosynclasticinfindimulum," and the rhythm of that word has lodged in my brain for over thirty years as musically as did Mary Poppin's "supercalifragilisticexpealodosis." I still smile at Vonnegut's imaginative precursor to Viagra in his novel *Slapstick*, a sexual practice referred to as "bookamaroo" where two people press the soles of their feet together for erotic thrills. Of course, he also became the master of transitions threaded throughout his novels, with the likes of, "So it goes, So be it, Hi Ho," and "Good for you," and my favorite, "If this isn't nice, I don't know what is."

Like Mark Twain, Vonnegut the humorist got more cynical as he aged. Two of his habits nearly did him in: smoking in bed—which started a fire in his home—and consuming a regular nightcap, a practice which helped him sleep so soundly it nearly turned him into toast. How tragic it is that he once felt so bad about the world where he lived that he attempted to take his own life. That he lived long enough (eighty-four) to be disappointed by humanity is not a surprise; that he still remained able to make readers laugh until the end constitutes a miracle.

I'D RATHER EAT CROW

Corvidae is a family of intelligent and mischievous birds, so it's no surprise that Jack Kisling chose a crow to perch so prominently in the title of his under-appreciated-and-therefore-not-so-bestseller, *The Crow Flies Crooked*. In this corner of the Four Corners region, many people have heard about it, but few have ever read it.

It is a difficult book to locate, but I got lucky. Kisling's first and only novel won second place in an important literary contest, the California Commonwealth Prize for fiction, but unfortunately that same year Pulitzer Prize winner Wallace Stegner just happened to submit his ninth book to the same contest, and it won first place. Bad timing.

Published in 1966 and never reprinted, Kisling's book chronicles a small town's devotion to stupidity, deceit, and a brand of pinto-bean-flavored poetic justice in a fictional location known as Crying Creek, just up or down the road from many small towns in America. Since I moved to my small town over thirty years ago, old-timers have whispered to me about the novel, how it qualifies as a thinly veiled libelous attack on living individuals. It has even been suggested that locals were so offended by the text, they gathered up all the copies they could find and burned them. As for how much truth exists in any of this, I can only report that if the book is scandalous, it's also hilarious.

A reviewer on Amazon that claims to have lived in these parts forty or so years ago penned these words: "Author Jack Kisling has accurately depicted the people in this little-known Colorado town, believe it or not. If the exact events aren't exactly as they happened, they might as well have been."

That may be so, but it's beside the point. Knowing who is allegedly depicted in this book does nothing but distract this reader and frankly, it turns a good novel like *The Crow Flies Crooked* into nothing more than yellow journalism. It also does a disservice to a talented author who populated his pages with the necessary cast to tell his particular story. No living persons were ever harmed during the typing of his manuscript. What's the big deal?

What Kisling accomplishes is to create an accurate portrayal of human nature, and the more precise that depiction is, the more likely someone is going to be offended. We see ourselves in shadows, and we are frightened (or in this case angered) at the recognition of our own shortcomings embedded on the page for everyone to see. When the characters of Tiny Elmore and Little Clint step into the story, for example, their appearance, interests, and mannerisms may remind us of actual people, but that doesn't make Kisling a biographer.

Fiction writers belong to a tier of lesser gods, semi-omnipotent to the extent that they are able to spin the raw and granulated events of ordinary life into cotton candy. Journalists are a different lot, more akin to the genus Corvus, the best of them skilled at gathering bits of fluff and shiny stuff so the prose sparkles when they write, but their stories are expected to fly in a straight line.

Jack Kisling spent thirty years in the business as a journalist for the *Denver Post* after leaving a rural newspaper editor post, but in that tiny tick of time known as "the interim," he penned his novel. Colleagues in the newspaper business respected his wit, his craft, and his companionship. He died in 1998 after a long struggle with brain cancer. His newspaper columns have predictably turned to ash in the incinerator of time, because news of the world's events burns hot at the moment it's written, then quickly cools.

The Crow Flies Crooked, however, deserves a grander audience. I've been hunting for a personal copy just to savor what I've already read, but as I said, it's hard to find. The book qualifies as a collectible, not because it's valued as literature, but because so few copies can be located. One book dealer told me he handled a signed copy a few years back and sold it for $50. I'd love to have been that buyer. Another dealer suggests that a copy might be located for $100. I could ask him to hunt that one down, although I wish the book came with a time machine so I'd be able to give the money directly to the author and shake his hand.

When (and if) I find my own copy, I should be clear about one thing: No, you can't borrow it, and you shouldn't ask. Book borrowers are the sort of characters who will show up in my first novel.

LIFE, THE UNIVERSE, AND ONE OTHER THING

"He felt that his whole life was some kind of dream and he sometimes wondered whose it was and whether they were enjoying it."
—Douglas Adams, *The Hitchhiker's Guide to the Galaxy*

A hammock is a time machine. I purchased mine cheap at the Wabi-sabi in Moab, Utah. Some guy named Eddie Bauer had stitched his name into the fabric, but that was alright with me. I have no problem traveling on Bauered time.

It feels like years since I first hitched up the contraption between two sturdy trees, the sun burning high above me in the Manti-La Sal National Forest. I grabbed my pillow before climbing in, and I would encourage other time travelers to do the same. Pillows help tremendously when dealing with the impact of time, even better than towels. The promontory where I camped overlooked the dilapidated remains of what must have been tiny houses in an uninhabited canyon. Far below, over a scramble of steep, rocky terrain I heard a rush of water, at a distance I did not plan to hike. I did, after all, own a time machine.

Sunlight filtered through the leaves, so the light flickered, almost like the same pillar of transporter energy I'd seen Scotty engage on countless reruns of *Star Trek*. I closed my eyes and I was gone.

Perhaps my molecules were reassembled in that other place, perhaps not, but my consciousness came to rest among the ruins of a real estate venture, an investment of a different time: The Home of Truth. The year was 1933.

I had driven past the ruins of the settlement on many occasions while driving into Canyonlands National Park. The place looked like the ruination of one of those themed dinner ranches where tourists pay to taste barbecue smoke while partying in the Old West. You know, cowboy songs and cowboy poetry, that sort of West.

In this time period, however, I had done a little research. A crimson veil fell across my eyes and I saw a colony of devout believers and their messiah, Mary Ogden, settling into the Dry Valley. Mrs. Ogden claimed to receive revelations directly from God through her typewriter. These revelations included a dogma that advocated reincarnation, resurrection, and a form of spiritualism involving vibrations, spiritual planes, soul language, conversations with the dead and other astro-esoteric notions. Nearly a hundred followers joined her by 1935, living communally, the same way where developers today design eco-friendly gated communities. Mary Ogden's Home of Truth was off the grid, but in an entirely different way.

Then I woke, understandably disoriented. The pleasure and the trouble with hammocks is that confounded rocking motion, which must also imitate the way we settle on the places where we decide to live. It's like a huge cosmic pendulum, back and forth, back and forth, never arriving or staying at a happy medium. Either we lull ourselves to sleep, believing any spot on the earth is ours for the taking, or we wake up with a thud, having fallen from grace and our visions of Eden, in a subdivision organized around a maze of shopping outlets.

Mrs. Ogden, I learned, organized her colony into three portals: The Outer, the Middle, and the Inner Portal—the one where she resided. She served as financial director for the colony, controlling all its decisions. She offered her followers eternal salvation if they handed over all their earthly assets.

The wind stopped blowing, my time machine stopped glowing. I sat up straight and a revelation came to me. I didn't even have a typewriter.

The key to understanding yourself is simple. Buy a hammock.

DESERT'S ELEVEN

When I find a used book that has been inscribed by its author, my heart flutters a bit and I get nervous and glance over my shoulder, just in case the cashier or store manager has noticed a surge in its market potential. But as we all know, not all signatures are equal. A signed first edition of *The Hobbit* with its original dust jacket was recently appraised on the Antiques Roadshow for between $80,000 and $100,000.

I recently acquired a Patti LaBelle cookbook. You remember, the singer Patti LaBelle and the Bluebelles? She'd autographed her book in a tasteful, cursive style on the title page with an ink that reminded me of either a homemade au jus or a crème brûlée.

Andy Nettell, the proprietor of Back of Beyond Books in Moab, Utah, clicked his tongue and moved his head from side to side, not questioning the signature's authenticity but rather, questioning my judgement for bringing this book into his inventory of collectible Southwest literature.

"But it's signed!" I exclaimed.

"Signed, but unsung" he replied.

Then he motioned me over to three stacks of books in glossy mylar covers and told me it took him nine months to talk this collector into selling. Every title, either by Edward Abbey or Tony Hillerman, was signed, no exception. Nearly fifty books. Patti LaBelle fluttered her eyelashes from the bottom of my cardboard box.

I own a couple of signed Tony Hillerman books too, copies I treasure and refuse to sell. I told my bookseller friend so, but he demurred.

"Hillerman signed so many books the value of the ink has been diluted for all but his early editions."

I also own many Edward Abbey books, most of them in paperback. I even commissioned a tapestry of Abbey by a local fabric artist that hangs over my desk, but Ed's ink—that earthy tincture of desert hue—still eludes me.

"May I peek at his signature?" Andy flipped open title page after title page, the dead man's scrawl, graceful and legible, so unlike the scruffy desert image of the man. Every signature accompanied by a date: Edward Abbey, 11/6/68; Edward Abbey, 11/16/80; Edward Abbey, 11/1/63, and so on.

"Isn't it odd that Abbey signed all these books in November?"

"I suspect he was just screwing with the public, once he found out his signature significantly increased the value of his books. He allegedly dated some of his inscriptions before the actual publication date, just to see if anyone would notice. I've still got to examine these books more closely."

But I'd seen enough. Abbey and I, for whatever reason, were drawn to the same number: eleven. For over forty years, as mysteriously as Deja vu, the digital devices I glance at display the numerals *11:11*. I don't know why I keep being drawn to look at clocks at that particular moment. For the longest time, I worried the recurrence might be a premonition of my own death, but I managed to get through 11 November 2011 unscathed—both a.m. and p.m. Now I wonder why Abbey chose the number eleven to say, in essence, I am here.

He wasn't born in November. He didn't die in November. Somehow the number eleven got into his psyche and he couldn't work it loose. Or didn't want to. It turned out to be his guilty pleasure, maybe even his little joke. Abbey convinced me at that moment standing in Andy's Moab bookstore that the number eleven should be my charm, not my curse.

The author Cormac McCarthy, another one of my favorites, is notorious for refusing to sign copies of his books. I own first editions, but no signatures. I asked the bookseller if he had a signed McCarthy in his shop and, if so, could I see the signature?

"Just one." He showed me a copy, the third book of McCarthy's Border trilogy, then he told me about an appraisal he'd done of a private collection where he encountered a copy of McCarthy's *Blood Meridian*, a valuable first edition book in itself, even unsigned. The copy he appraised had been inscribed by Cormac McCarthy—of all persons—to Edward Abbey, dated from a time long before McCarthy had made his mark in the annals of literature, a whooping twenty-two years before he was awarded a Pulitzer Prize for *The Road*.

"Wow," I said, but what I meant was that in my book, on a scale of one to ten, that signature was easily an eleven.

I had to leave my box of books with the Andy, and he promised to sort through my stuff when he returned from the California International Antiquarian Book-fair in Pasadena. Then he'd mail me a check for the titles he could use. I suspected he'd be taking Patti LaBelle with him, if not for the sale, then just for the company.

ONE LAST HURRAH

One Labor Day, I found myself in Las Vegas, a vacation destination known for buffet lines, not picket lines. Turning a corner beside The Cosmopolitan, I heard bullhorns blaring protest slogans while hundreds of people lofting signs formed a human barricade in front of the hotel and casino, all of them wearing red T-shirts, responding to their union's call to strike.

"Tasteless," was the comment I overheard from a bystander. I laughed out loud. He gave me a dirty look, then moved off, not a clue as to how appropriately his single word editorial captured the dissatisfaction of the 44,000-member culinary workers' union that had voted to walk away from the table.

Jimmy Hoffa probably dreamt about picket lines, for he'd started his career as a young union activist, became a successful organizer, and ultimately was elected to serve as president of this nation's largest collective bargaining group, the Teamsters. He was also convicted of fraud, attempted bribery, and jury tampering, receiving a thirteen-year prison sentence, of which he only served four years, because Richard Nixon pardoned him in 1971.

"One, two, three, four, don't go through that hotel door"—a rhyme for solidarity, urging tourists to boycott the casino. The picket signs danced, reminding me of 1981, the year I signed my first teaching contract in Minnesota, the first year as a professional I paid any union dues.

That year also served as my first experience with a strike when the teachers' union called for a walkout over contract issues I didn't even understand. Further negotiations eventually resolved the impasse, and I followed my fellow unionists back to work.

I believed in unions then, in the power of employees to join together and stand up for each other, to be treated fairly, to be heard in the larger arena where management decisions affected workers' livelihoods. My little classroom was a cog in the great wheel of educational well-being, and I felt proud to have joined ranks with my teaching colleagues.

That spring, just as the hard feelings started to soften, next year's contracts were delivered. Instead of a contract, I received a letter informing me that my job had been eliminated due to a "reduction in forces." My colleagues told me I'd been riffed. Fired? No, just not rehired, but I wanted to know why. My evaluations were acceptable. I called my representative and told him what happened. He already knew, and he said there was nothing the union could do.

I asked if I got fired because I joined in the walkout. He said probably. I asked if the school board could do that. He said yes, adding that non-tenured teachers could be dismissed for any reason, or for no reason. I demanded that the union file some kind of complaint on my behalf. I had, after all, paid my dues.

I even thought about making trouble, but then I remembered James Riddle Hoffa, the union boss that disappeared. Over thirty-nine years later, we still have no idea what happened to him, or rather, where his body ended up, because it's unlikely he moved to a resort in South America. Sixty-seven percent of those surveyed at Debate.org believe labor unions have outlived their usefulness, citing the enactment of tougher labor laws, redundancy, expense, and corruption as the biggest reasons for the slump in popularity. In a recent Gallup poll, the labor union reputation does not fare much better. Although respondents generally approve, a majority of people believe unions are weaker and of less importance than in their heyday, and over eighty percent of households have no family member that belongs to a union.

The most depressing aspect of labor union history is that many of our youth have probably never heard of Jimmy Hoffa, but today's workforce has a growing need to address an agenda of work-related grievances, like minimum wage, the nebulous nature of company health insurance, and the artificial status of part-time positions imposed by bosses to reduce worker benefits. Just like locating Hoffa's remains, we seem to have stopped looking for answers.

Perhaps what we need is a tombstone planted in every cemetery across America, engraved with the words "Jimmy Hoffa Might Be Here." And people would start asking, who was this Hoffa guy? And maybe then we'll be able to dig deeper for a better explanation about why on the first Monday of every September America takes the weekend off.

AN URNING WAGE

T he thing young people never expect to find in a thrift store is their parents, and I don't mean just any elderly couple strolling the aisles reminiscing over items they used to own. Parents, especially retired ones living on fixed incomes, appreciate thrift stores offering regular senior discounts. By now you are probably imagining sweet old people holding hands in a second-hand shop, searching for bargains. But no, the couple I'm referring to sat quietly on a shelf in two polished and permanently sealed funeral urns.

Seriously. I picked them up and felt the heft of ash shift inside. I tipped them to peek at their bottoms where a volunteer had scribbled a price. Six dollars. E ach.

To be clear, these were not my parents, nor may they have been anyone's parents I have ever met, but I assure you they were two expensive cremation urns with three to five pounds of a loose powdery something inside—what I know to be the approximate weight of an incinerated corpse, minus pocket change. I carefully placed them back on the shelf, puzzled by what I'd found.

Mark Twain characterized the hereafter as "Heaven for climate, hell for society." Where ending up in a thrift store fits between these options is hard to say. A sympathy welled up inside me. I felt like handing the money over and taking these unwitting eternities home with me, maybe hammering their lids loose and scattering their remains in more traditional locations like beautiful meadows, shimmering lakes or rivers, or emptying them over the edge of a ruggedly alluring cliff. It would have been the proper thing to do, because all cultures seem to agree that the dead deserve our respect.

As I stepped back and sat on a slightly worn but perfectly serviceable couch that was itself hoping for a second life, I pondered what to do. I watched another customer pick up one of the urns, cursorily examine it, and return it to the shelf. Moving six feet to the left, she leaned forward to look deeply into a bathroom vanity mirror, as if testing the temperature of a quiet pond by touching its surface with one finger, then she wandered away. Soon, a young man grabbed an urn and held it up to the light before putting it back. No sale. Life moves on.

The thought of spending eternity in a thrift store prompted me to consider the many residents that wildfire evacuations temporarily displace from their homes. I can hardly imagine returning home after fire containment and finding an all too poignant future reduced to ash. It must feel like an eternity. Thankfully a natural optimism resides in trees and given time, forests can anticipate a new life.

Our own fate is more subject to speculation. The average funeral today costs just under ten thousand dollars, which partly explains why almost half of the dying opt for a slightly less expensive cremation. Besides, I would have felt less comfortable finding two sealed coffins pushed up against this couch in the furniture section.

To my delight, a friend related a memorable experience when I told my tale about finding the urns. His experience helped me put a funeral home's excessive add-on expenses associated with death into perspective.

Funeral home personnel quoted a price of about $400 to purchase an urn. Can't be helped, my friend thought, but while sorting his relative's household to dispose of her worldly goods he discovered a beautiful piece of stoneware. He called the funeral home to ask if a piece of loved pottery could serve as an urn. Reluctantly, the funeral manager agreed, but apprised him of the legal requirement for putting any pottery in a burial box if it is be placed in the ground. My friend asked how much? About $400 was the reply. While continuing the excavation of his aunt's belongings, he came across a surprisingly serviceable metal storage trunk. Would that heirloom do for containment? He called. Hesitantly, the substitution was approved.

How these two cremation urns turned up at the thrift store may have a completely reasonable explanation, but I'm not sure I want to know. Until someone involved in the matter writes me a letter with another good story, I've decided that ending up where you never expected may be a happy alternative to our streamlined rest-in-peace industry. After all, as I witnessed while sitting across from my mystery couple, the living are still inclined to hold you, sometimes tenderly, or they gently upend your complacency by shifting your powdered bones like sand in an hourglass. I wouldn't be opposed to a little more of this kind of existence before moving on to the greater and unquotable unknown.

GRATITUDE ODE

I nstead of exchanging corny greeting cards for our anniversary, we celebrated by traveling to Winchester, England. John Keats's fondness for a footpath through the St. Cross meadows is part of his legacy, and for two months we walked that path almost every day. Of the meadows he wrote, "There is on one side of the city a chalky down where the air is worth sixpence a pint." After returning to the cheap lodging he shared with his best friend in the fall of 1819, he penned his famous ode, "To Autumn."

An ode is a literary outpouring of respect or gratitude for the subject at hand and Keats wrote many odes. Once, after boasting of habitually sleeping until 10:00 a.m., he composed an "Ode to Indolence." His most famous poems are in this style: "Ode to a Nightingale," "Ode to a Grecian Urn," "Ode to Psyche," and although it sounds awkwardly aligned with an ode's purpose, also an "Ode to Melancholy."

Two hundred twenty-five years later—and also in the fall—we also visited Winchester, where we retraced Keats's footsteps, and strolled appreciatively beside the same stream. I admired the lush pastoral scenery, stopping to watch a pair of swans preening their snow-white feathers, counting sheep grazing in the meadow, wondering if he had stepped in the same muck we so narrowly avoided.

But that's as far as my reverie got. My bare leg brushed against a patch of nettles and the pain was instant. It felt like a dozen bees had suddenly stung me. I hopped around on the narrow path, rubbing my calf until I lost my balance and backed right into another nettles patch.

I could have blamed the entire irritating experience on Keats, but as a seventy-one-year-old writer with a tenderness for poetic justice, I should have known better. The river that feeds this chalk stream is, after all, appropriately named the Itchen.

Today, the Wildlife Trust maintains St. Cross Meadow, a nature reserve that offers streams, meadows, and wet woodland to sustain a diverse wildlife. It is gorgeous, but in 1819 its untamed character also inspired Keats to draft letters to his many friends, recommending in an outpouring of good-natured words that they, "pass across St Cross meadows till you come to the most beautifully clear river—now this is only one mile of my walk, I will spare you the other two till after supper when they would do you more good."

These days, wandering off the meadow path requires you to cross a sporting field, tennis court, and parking lot—that is, if you can ignore the polite postings that forbid climbing over any fences and urging visitors to Please Stay on the Footpath. But the stream is still like glass, so clear the white chalk shimmers from the bottom.

Because chalk is permeable, water percolates easily through the ground to the water table, so chalk streams receive little surface runoff. Fewer than three hundred chalk rivers have been identified globally, and eighty-five percent of them are located in southern England. As a retired teacher who has spent considerable time with a piece of chalk in hand, I couldn't help reaching into the stream, picking up a pebble and tracing a few swirly white lines on a flat rock beside me. But an ode to chalk it was not.

Keats saw his early writing flourish, but his finances suffered. Giving up a medical career to become a poet hadn't helped. He published three volumes of verse and numerous magazine articles in just four short years, but much of his work was received indifferently by the literary establishment during his lifetime. Like talented creative artists everywhere, he had to die to become famous.

I picture Keats not only roaming the meadow but also spending considerable time inside Winchester Cathedral, absorbing its history and epitaphs, sitting in a corner scribbling notes, even standing beside a recent memorial to a forty-one-year-old little-known novelist named Jane Austen, a writer who also found fame only after she died—two years before Keats arrived in the city.

Like Keats, Austen, too, had come to Winchester to receive medical treatment, and she stayed in a house only a stone's throw away from the cathedral. None of her six anonymously published novels were in print at the time of her death, although Keats—who read and studied both history and literature— surely had encountered news of her as a novelist.

Austen was laid to rest in Winchester Cathedral in 1817. Keats, just twenty-five, was buried in Rome four years later, seventeen months after leaving Winchester, having been advised by his physician to move to a warmer climate. What he found in Rome, I don't know, but I like to think his ramblings through "our" meadow remained vivid in his memory. For his beguiling words and for pointing out the path, I will always be grateful, but never for his nettles.

THE ROAD TO OBLIVION

C ombined with my nearly illegible handwriting, putting directions on paper can't help but get the anxious traveler hopelessly confused. Just go north of Morgan's Tower along the Devil's Highway to Crying Creek, then straight toward oblivion. It sounds fairly simple to me.

The wanderer is probably unfamiliar with my geographical references and has no context to build an accurate mental map. Unfortunately, GPS is also useless, because many of these locations truly represent oblivion, for they've been obscured by time.

Even if I try to be more precise: head north from Cortez, Colorado (the town first settled at an old stage stop and ancient ruin complex called Mitchell Springs, where Morgan's Tower once stood, described by archaeologist Lewis Henry Morgan as a ten or twelve-foot mound that was bulldozed by pot hunters in 1977) along Highway 491 (sometimes formerly referred to as

"The Devil's Highway," because it was Highway 666 back then, just a spur off the infamous Route 66 that attracted a wave of American tourism) where you'll encounter an agrarian community known as Dove Creek (fictionally renamed Crying Creek in Jack Kisling's 1966 novel titled *The Crow Flies Crooked*, which, was not appreciated by the Creek's local residents at the time of its publication), you'll wish you'd headed toward oblivion and skipped the encounter with me.

Time is like an unrelenting wind unraveling a shroud of sand, erasing any tracks, leaving the surface smooth and apparently untraveled.

What I love about the route north from Cortez to Monticello is the sheer number of tiny, deserted houses that populate its roadside horizons like drowsy withered sunflowers, the houses originally seeded by an early-to-mid-twentieth century agricultural push that populated this stretch of land with families. These days, a driver flying along at sixty-five miles an hour has to really scrutinize the roadside horizons in order to notice the tiny houses. In tallying these lost hopes, I've arrived at more than I could count on my fingers and toes.

A portfolio of black and white images, ambitiously titled *North of Cortez on the Way to Oblivion*, would provide a fascinating history—each abandoned house telling its own little story.

But after two decades considering such a project, I've given the idea up. The knowledge of the families that lived in these rickety residences has frayed like cobwebs against the hands of unrelated generations. The houses are mostly decrepit crumbling artifacts, often isolated in the middle of a farmer's field where trespassing is especially *verboten*, a word that still resonates with the impact a gun's hammer makes after being cocked and pointed in my direction.

Another detail that strikes me as arresting is the size of these "family" houses. North Americans have gained on average one-to-three inches in height in the last century, but their house sizes have nearly tripled since 1950. It won't be helpful to discuss how our breadth has also increased, an obesity index ticking upward since 1950 from ten percent to thirty-five percent of the population, so I'm not going there, because we're all heading toward an oblivion of our own making. The journey, after all, will always be my official answer to the eternal question that asks, what is the meaning of life? Besides, there's an enormous difference between examining old photographs and encountering the actual shambles of our collective history. The past has so often been a straightforward "thanks for the memories," and a glance over the shoulder on its way out the door. True appreciation, however, is like a favorite shirt you're afraid to wash because somehow you just know it will change, shrink, fade, wrinkle, or unravel in a horrible, irrecoverable way.

And it will, count on it. Sometimes I just pull off the highway, sit on the shoulder with my hazard lights flashing, and simply pause for what Paddington Bear calls "a hard stare," or "a long view." With my spotting scope zoomed and focused, my eye approaches the broken front door to ask permission and when not even a shadow answers, my magnified eye slips around to the side of the house, examines the openings where window glass once held out the rain, and then I'll take a sweeping tour around the yard to count the trees and flowers before I put the scope away and move along. When I stop, it's a comfort, like a visit with neighbors I seldom get to see.

One spring I spotted a pair of fruit trees in full blossom outside the backdoor at one of these abandoned houses and I swear I could hear the bees swarming, buzzing in their frantic effort to harvest and stockpile a cupboard full of nectar. Then, the sound merged with the traffic, which I had so completely forgotten as it sped past my idling car. In that instant, there was no difference between the bees and the motorized scurry of constant change. I should have closed my eyes and visited oblivion, but it was late and I had to be getting home.

4: VISIT YOUR "PUBLIC" LANDS

A DELICATE MATTER

At Delicate Arch, the Park Service stresses the importance of carrying water, staying on the trail, wearing appropriate shoes, and leaving no trace. What it never mentions is that hikers like me should keep snide remarks about the throngs of other hikers to themselves. I wanted to say something to the woman heading up a steep incline with her newborn infant joggling in a sling against her chest, and to the parents of a towhead without a hat running full tilt along a crest of slick rock, and to the couple passionately making out in the narrow slip of shade along a rock face, but I didn't. Instead, I just grabbed my water bottle and sucked it up.

Because I'm not in Arches National Park right now, it might be appropriate to touch lightly upon some of the impulses I suppressed while sharing the rock, so to speak, with more than a few of my fellow aliens—judging by the otherworldly ways in which we conduct ourselves.

Let me start by mentioning the intensity of the human voice. In my opinion, sports arenas are the proper venue for shouting, screaming, yelling, and generally letting loose at decibel levels that shatter the natural world. The one-and-a-half mile route from Wolfe Ranch to Delicate Arch is not a marathon, or any other kind of sporting event. Folks set their own pace with a goal of reaching the most recognizable and popular arch in the park just to see its magnificence. Nobody wins if a someone's voice arrives before the body.

Another matter worth pursuing now that I'm feeling freer to express myself is the difference between petroglyphs and graffiti. Both are accomplished by carving on soft sandstone walls with a hard instrument, and each is sponsored by a human desire to prove that we exist.

The difference? It's the amount of time, that's all. In early April, a hiking spot near Sand Dune Arch had to be closed by park officials because a few of the over one-million annual visitors defaced the rock surfaces with their personal cries for permanence. Contributions like the declaration that AL+BF, scratched inside the shape of a heart, give banality a bad name. Nothing the ancestors left behind on rock walls bears any testimony to their personal egos. No BF deal to them, but for some reason, the selfie of our culture continues to assert itself.

I would recommend that hikers focus on their *pedroglyphs* along the trail—namely, the personal tread patterns imprinted in the soft dirt when there is enough dirt to snatch the ghost of their stride from the bottoms of their feet, if that could only satisfy the urge to leave a mark on the earth.

Much of the Delicate Arch trail traverses rock. Its surface has been scoured by weather for eons, long before humans, or aliens, ever found their footing in the earth's ecosystem. The park boasts over two thousand natural arches in its catalog, carved by the pointy tip of time. Geology doesn't chew gum and spit it out along the trail. It doesn't leave sweatshirts hanging on convenient limbs or posts or toss empty plastic water bottles in the shallow indentations where rainwater pools. These are the manifestations of a manifest destiny.

The parking lot, like the bottom of an hourglass, continually fills with vehicles until every designated space is occupied. The Park Service (not to be confused with any kind of valet parking service) recommends that if a particular lot is full, visitors should return at a later time, which is not what happens when other vehicles pull in, unable to find a parking place. They begin to circle the lot like petroleum-based buzzards, or they stop and idle, air conditioners blasting, waiting for someone's time to expire.

If a person should be so lucky as to reach the informal amphitheater where Delicate Arch occupies center stage, a crowd of resting figures will likely never notice that one more creature has arrived. A hundred cameras will be loading that arch, pixel by pixel, onto their memory cards. Children will be chasing the chipmunks that scamper and then hide in the most convenient rock crevice. The sun will reveal its own trajectory of a massive arch from one horizon to the other, heating the rock surface along the way, reminding everyone that time is light, or energy, or atoms, or some absurd variation of all the forces beyond anyone's control— including human behavior.

ANOTHER GRAND CANYON

A popular tourist feature at the south rim of Black Canyon National Park is Chasm overlook. Across the canyon, I spotted a railing that protects sightseers from taking a fatal step off its north rim. Not even a quarter mile of thin air separated us, but the promise of the two-thousand-foot plummet contained all the encouragement I needed just to smile and wave.

Congress upgraded the Black Canyon by designating it a national park in 1999, sixty-six years after President Herbert Hoover first declared it a national monument. I asked a friend of mine, a retired park service superintendent, what was the difference between the two? He told me that generally national monuments have a single natural feature that attracts visitors, whereas a national park contains more than just one. I see, I said, but I didn't. He must have sensed my confusion, so he added, "Mostly it's just politics."

Although Black is a grand canyon, it's not *the* Grand Canyon. Nearly five million visitors stop by annually to look over its edge and say, "wow," but to visit the Black Canyon, you have to want to go there. It's not just a detour to a colossal crack in the desert you encounter while traveling to or from Disneyland. It requires some backroad planning.

Standing at the precipice, I heard the Black Canyon call to me, subliminally, from beneath the river's roar. I had never been to the north side, and it beckoned me to cross. In the thirty years I've lived in Colorado, I've only visited this national park once, and for me time is trickling away. For the canyon, where a billion-year-old Precambrian rock tooth glistens in a slip of sunlight, reaching the canyon's bottom, time is not such a big deal.

Or it could be those folks waving from the north rim that inspired me. No bridge to span the canyon has ever been built, and thankfully imagination always falls short, so driving was my only option. The park brochure recommended allotting two hours for the trip.

The north rim road twists like black licorice, and the view is sweet. Although the way is narrow, it's not as harrowing as the canyon itself. I pulled in at every available vantage point for a look and a photograph. You see, there's nothing so inspiring as depth. (We scratch the surface for most of the days of our lives. If we get the chance to look over the edge, we should not forget to take a deep breath and be inspired.)

I was once surprised to learn Robert Frost's roots make him a westerner, because he was born in California, but he is known as a rural New England poet. At age eleven, he moved to Massachusetts to live in his grandfather's house following his father's sudden death. His geography changed, and a rift in his young life altered his perspective. Had he grown up in his native West, I believe his famous poem, "Stopping by Woods on a Snowy Evening," would never have seen any snow and ended something like this: ""these canyons are lovely, dark and deep, but I have promises to keep, and miles to go before I sleep, and miles to go before I sleep."

During my trip to the north rim, that verse echoed in my brain like a song that you can't stop humming.

Over four hours later—not the prescribed two—I came full circle, back to the Chasm overlook where I had started, my odometer having clocked 185 miles. The evening shadows had just started their descent to the canyon floor. The only energy I had left was to make my way to the south rim campground and open a cold beer. Lucky for me, I hadn't made any other promises.

EMILY POST–ITS

I don't know if it was proper to make a gift out of something somebody else threw away. It was just a book, a 1945 edition of Emily Post's *Etiquette*, with its dust jacket more or less intact. I'm a guy who's fond of recycling. I also refused to wrap it before I gave the book to my friend who loves to laugh at the way things used to be.

For 654 packed pages, Emily (or I should say, Mrs. Post) tries to clarify every conceivable confusion about proper behavior in a constantly changing world, from "Mrs. Three-in-One Gives a Party" to "Telephoning, Smoking, and Out-In-Company Manners." She notes that the text for her book has been "completely rewritten . . . because the problems of modern life demand certain changes in the forms of living." Ah, if Mrs. Post could see us now.

Of course, maybe a book like this still has a place in our time, despite today's readers feeling a little thick about what constitutes decency. Awkward and just plain thoughtless behavior still exists. When was the last time a 4X4 monster truck parked a front tire up on the curb of the sidewalk where you're walking, or you were forced to listen to an RV's generator while snuggled in your sleeping bag beneath a canopy of stars? Even by doubling the number of pages, would Emily have had sufficient room to say what needs saying about the way we conduct our Post-modern social affairs?

An etiquette for the West, if that's possible, should probably be uploaded to YouTube if Westerners are ever to be exposed to it. However, Post-It notes would be more efficient for me, and for other people on the go: an *Emily Post-It Guide to Rude Behavior*. You see, it's not so much the accumulation of etiquette knowledge that's important; rather, it's the ability to stick what you know in, or literally on, somebody else's face. "American Idol," "The Apprentice," Judge Judy, Don Imus, and Dr. Phil are all symptoms of a societal infection that rages within us: the desire to tell people off in the most public arena possible. Quick access to the right thing to say could be a Post-It plus.

Vehicles, for example, pose us with a new challenge for polite behavior. Emily's advice on chauffeur etiquette might easily be updated in my new Post-It edition with a few of the following sticky notes:

Dirt becomes you. My Ram's bigger than your Ram. My horse trailer looks like your RV.

Another chapter that might be ripped right out of Emily's big blue book is the one titled "Table Manners." My Post-It edition will use the heading "Manners-to-go":

Your burger has my number on it. This table cleaned by the previous customer's sleeve. Caution: chewing tobacco produces secondhand spit.

I scoured Emily's fourteen-page index to find some reference to outdoor etiquette, but apparently people's behavior in 1945 was so class-driven that the rules for engaging the natural world had an unearthly feel about them. Instead of trying to negotiate an equitable means for motorized and non-motorized enthusiasts to share wilderness trails, Emily points out that shorts are still only "proper for the young and slim;" that older women are strongly advised to choose their bathing suits with the word "ample" in mind, and that the thought of bare-toed sandals with evening dresses is "too revolting to mention" (although she does, of course, mention it). Today, the bigger the size the wider the eyes.

I want to know if it's proper to talk on a cell phone while standing in a cliff dwelling, if kicking trail cairns over, trashing restrooms, tagging rock faces in the back country, or tossing cigarette butts out car windows are behaviors society should tolerate. Maybe we need a new public land motto: "Take only memories, leave only sticky notes." You see, I can't control what people wear, but they wear me down with their rude and obnoxious attitudes toward the natural world. If it ever was truly important to treat each other with excruciating respect, then it's doubly important to treat our public lands with an even greater regard.

The book I gave away contains a black and white photo of a uniformed maid, tray balanced on one hand, posing before a partially opened door. It is captioned with this tiny bit of pre-Post-It wisdom: "[The house] may be of no size at all, but its details are perfect, and its bell is answered promptly by a trim maid with a low voice and quiet, courteous manner." Naturally, I was tempted to draw a mustache on her upper lip before giving the book away, but in her long-winded style Emily is unintentionally correct: This mansion made of earth could always use a few more servants.

RECREATIONAL 'NOITERING

While swatting gnats in the shade of a tall piñon tree at New Mexico's Datil Well Campground, I couldn't help smiling as the driver of a forty-foot luxury motorhome towing a spare vehicle on a flatbed trailer 'noitered the campground loop for a parking space. I say 'noitered because the intentional misspelling of a word has always been an author's prerogative. Reconnoiter is the proper word, but the girth of his reality did not bode well for finding a suitable berth. 'Noitering feels more playful, more animated, like a television game show. I sat back in my comfortable front row seat.

After the third trip around the loop he pulled into a meandering dirt track with thick stands of junipers on both sides. It wasn't a designated site. He must have been trying to avoid the sharp cornering required for occupying a nearby site.

I'd been keen for some entertainment. When I arrived the previous day, the thermometer displayed 98 degrees in the shade with a "Boil Water" notice attached to the pump handle. A few other peasant campers had landed since then. One was also paying attention from across the loop and she smiled toward me, as spectators often do.

I hope nobody takes issue with my suggestion, that America could use an agility competition for the drivers of huge recreational motorhomes and fifth-wheel trailers, because I realize most BLM and Forest Service campgrounds already offer sufficient unintended challenges that can eventually refine anyone's backup skills. The huge rolling motels might be better off in sites that private RV parks offer, where electricity, sewer, and water are available, and one just happened to be in business down the road, although likely not as economical as the Datil fee of $5 per night.

The small town of Datil is populated by about fifty residents, one gas station with a good cafe and a scattering of tired houses just off Highway 60. I imagine the community could use a boost in tourist revenue by hosting a competitive event like The Annual New Mexico 'Noitering Championship. In fact, every state in the union might be happy to host its own qualifying event, sending its best-skilled driver to a national championship. There are plenty of qualifying dryland flagships on the road.

1. The rules would be simple: Only two classes may compete, motorhomes or fifth-wheels, forty feet or longer. Vehicles towing an additional vehicle, boat, or trailer will be awarded a handicap.

2. Only the most unsuitable public land campgrounds for parking these large rigs may host an annual qualifying round, and only one event per state.

A national championship competition will test each state's best backer-upper for the top prize. Speed and agility will be what determines the winner.

Speaking of backing up, the rig that pulled into the meandering dirt track next to me illustrates the complexity of the contest. In this example, the driver could not move forward without dragging the side of his motorhome against the trees, nor backward without jackknifing the flatbed trailer. Harming a tree or detaching a trailer to simplify the task would disqualify the contestant. In this case, the campground host eventually walked over to explain parking was only allowed in designated campground sites, then kindly helped the driver resolve his predicament. Any advice by officials or spectators would be strictly prohibited. In this case, a wife finally emerged from the motorhome, but only walked over to a picnic table and held her head in her hands. No penalty would have applied.

Later that evening, just past dusk, another forty-footer—this time a fifth-wheel—circled the loop and stopped in the road, his diesel engine left idling, as if considering the open site kitty-corner from mine. I'd been staring at the moon but this spectacle suddenly was far more fascinating. The driver eventually exited his vehicle with a spotlight to inspect a narrow gravel strip, a behavior that would be considered wise and perfectly acceptable during a competition. Parking something this large in the dark, well, not so wise. Only natural light, such as a full moon or fireflies, would be acceptable.

After a half-dozen attempts—false reverses, pulling forward, realigning, and trying again—the driver finally managed to park his fifth-wheel in the slot. A half-dozen campers were standing beside the loop road, watching. One lady walked over and I overheard her congratulating the driver.

"Never thought you'd make it!" she exclaimed. Unfortunately, the front end of his truck still protruded, partially blocking the loop. After a few minutes of low-throated grumbles from an idling diesel engine, he pulled out again and vanished.

We were all impressed, although I suspect even the most open-minded of us, waving and wishing the driver a good berth, still whispered a titanic prayer like "preferably not anywhere near me."

SNEAKING INTO OUR PUBLIC LANDS

A young man strapped for cash arrived very late at a California campground forty years ago. He intended to leave very early, before the gate personnel showed up for work. A patch of dry ground near a small stream made a comfortable impromptu site, the soft sand a perfect mattress. He listened as a trickle of water played like a harp until he fell asleep.

Unfortunately the feeble rays of sunrise did not rouse him, but the sound of a nickering horse three feet from his ear did the trick. A stern male voice like old-time television's Mr. Ed commanded him to climb out of his sleeping bag. He opened his eyes and saw a mounted ranger staring down from his saddle at the bundle of his dreams. When he finally sat up the ranger announced, "You have failed at picking a campsite."

All these years later, I vividly remember that young man, because he was me. The memory persists. I slept very well. The ranger pointed with his outstretched arm toward a graveled area at least a hundred yards away, not anywhere near my sweet little stream. I promised to move at once. He told me he'd be back to see that I did. That's when I rolled and packed my gear, grabbed my backpack, and executed my one and only great escape from a national park.

Of America's 407 national park units, I have visited only seventy-seven, although several more often than once. Aside from that one time, I have dutifully stopped at every entrance station and paid my required user fee. I won't get more specific about the park's location in California for fear my Senior Pass might be revoked. Just imagine, being given approximately 84.4 million acres of America's most treasured heritage for my sixty-second birthday. Best gift ever.

When my birthday came around, any U.S. citizen who reached age sixty-two was permitted, for a one-time fee of $10, permanent free access to most of the park system's facilities where user fees are typically applied. I had worried for years that politicians would do away with the program before I reached my golden age. In 2007, for example, administrators at the National Park Service decided on a cosmetic change, ridding itself of the elegant name for its popular Golden Age Passport and adopting the generic term, Senior Pass, by which the program is known today.

No big deal you might think, but during my over-the-hill forties I was sure Congress would simply reduce the fees for seniors each time they entered a park. I can, after all, go to a thrift store and get a ten percent senior discount on Tuesdays, eat off the senior menu at many restaurants, or qualify for a cheap oil change. Perks for the elderly are nice, but they pale when compared with the privilege of receiving unobstructed access to our public lands.

Yellowstone achieved the status of becoming what is popularly acknowledged as America's first national park in 1872. Later, the 1906 Antiquities Act granted presidents the power to set land aside in the public's interest, designating unique acreage for protection as, say, a national monument. Since then, sixteen presidents from both parties have exercised their authority to protect America's heritage. Only one has sought to attack it.

Public lands face continuous threats far greater than young men sneaking into them without paying entrance fees. Partisan politics pushed the 2014 Republican-controlled House to send legislation on to the Senate limiting the president's authority to add exceptional cultural and natural beauty into the nation's land bank for posterity. H.R.1459 was never passed by the Senate. Now, a growing movement seeks the transfer of federal title on some public lands to local control. It worries me more than taking away my Senior Pass. My own county commissioners, along with many others, anted up thousands of taxpayer dollars to join the lobbying efforts of the Utah-based American Lands Council. Talk about sneaking into our public lands without paying fees!

To me, it's gratifying that upon leaving office our presidents have seen fit to endow the public with a sense of history too easily forgotten. Left up to business interests, the public would be granted acres of coal and oil fields, gravel pits, and shopping strips. Wall Street's insistence on unrestricted profit has already created an economic preserve for the wealthy that should not be confused with America's purple mountain majesties.

I look forward to the completion of every presidential term, and not just because of political antagonism. I blow out the candles and simply wish for a new parcel of public land. As our nation ages, we need more places for our expanding population, not just to see how America was, but to imagine how beautiful it could still be.

FEE-LOADING

We'd grumbled but nonetheless paid a nearly fifty percent fee increase for registering our Colorado motor vehicle as well as the registration fee for our camp trailer, which also nearly doubled. I felt as helpless as Jack, of beanstalk fame, hiding under a bucket while having to listen to a giant stomp around him shouting, *fee-fi-fo-fum!*

Fees paid, we decided to go camping at our favorite state park on Colorado's Western Slope. We paid our entrance fee and started looking around for a good camp site before getting hit up for the overnight camping fee. Then my wife gave me the news:

"Guess what? "I sighed: "Don't tell me there's a toilet paper fee. "No, I saw a motorhome with a toad threaten to turn a park ranger into a dwarf." Let me explain: When a motor home pulls a vehicle, the attachment is referred to as a toad, so last year Colorado state parks required the driver to pay the vehicle entrance fee twice—

once for the motor home, and a second time for the toad being towed. Many other states did and do the same. But our trailer has no engine. It's not a toad, nor are fifth-wheels, horse trailers or pop-up campers. These require no additional fees, and there's so little left in this culture that doesn't come with a fee that I felt like kissing my trailer, appropriately named a Scamp. But I didn't want to kiss the toad. No telling what it would turn into. RVers were justifiably upset, which is why the motorhome owner was berating the ranger. Doubling the entrance fee per day for some rigs that seem like two can be a tough act to follow.

The policy of charging a daily use fee on top of a camping fee is just the same rabbit coming out of a different hat. It might make better sense if the Chinese bought all our motorhomes, like they did with all our Hummers, but what can I say? I'm Scamping instead of tenting.

We have become a culture of fee-loaders, which is not that different from freeloaders. By definition, a free-loader is "a person who takes advantage of others' generosity without giving anything in return." Colorado state parks, for instance, have decided—according to park officials—to stave off funding deficits by "program reductions, small fee increases, and shorter hours at certain state parks." More fees, fewer services. Sounds like fee-loading to me.

Such tactics for increasing revenue are being used all across the West, and Colorado state parks are only following the same corporate model that sectors of American business have been abusing for generations. It amounts to this kind of thinking: generate more revenue by reducing the quality of the product, then pass an illusion of innovation on to the consumer, which is why we often find goods and even federal agencies repackaged and relabeled as "new and improved." I wouldn't be surprised if campers all across America eventually find their sites reclassified as "suites," requiring additional fees if campers occupy both the sleeping and the campfire areas of their dirt.

I can also imagine a strategy that breaks down the concept of fees into their components. When you see a park sign, you are assessed a recognition fee, which helps pay the rising cost of advertising for our tourism dollars. When you enter the park, you are charged an hourly use fee, which offsets the hourly salary all park employees are still required by law to be paid. Naturally, there will be an overnight fee if you intend to stay, and if you use water provided by the park, a water fee may be applicable. Toilet fees would be impractical, because nobody wants to encourage random peeing in the woods.

Maybe the problem with living in a fee-enriched economy is forgetting that the public is growing fee weary. We are all towing that economic toad, and brother, it's heavy.

Isn't it time someone concluded that a fee increase ought to come with some kind of improvement in product or service? I like the advertised image of staying at our local parks as if I were camping in my own backyard, but really, I paid my latest county tax assessment and I'm already being charged an additional fee to park in my own driveway. Fee-free at last, that is my new mantra.

SEISMIC EVENTS

Ah, Yellowstone! Although I hadn't been there since 1965, the excitement of having visited stays with me. The geyser, yeah, I saw that, and my father took pictures of me beside various rocks and trees, but what I remember most, much to his chagrin, was discovering a fondness for a girl who stayed with her parents at the Old Faithful Inn where we were registered, the first girl I'd ever felt that way about. Hormonally speaking, I'd probably reached the age when mating matters, and since then, according to my own national-park version of a Kinsey Report, every ninety-two minutes or so I think about Yellowstone.

I can't remember the girl's name, but I know we corresponded for a short time after returning from our family vacations, and I know this because my father fumed, calling me "girl crazy," while my siblings teased me about the experience, and teasing also stays with you. One of us eventually stopped writing, and that was that.

So I don't know what got into me, deciding to take a trip to Yellowstone nearly half century after that seminal experience. Perhaps with my hormonal levels finally adjusted, I began to wonder about all the natural beauty I missed at the fourth most visited national park in the nation.

Technically, an "old flame" is still at the bottom of it but calling it a "fumarole" would be more specific. Basically, a fumarole is an opening in the surface of the earth's crust associated with volcanic lesions that emit various gases and steam. Yellowstone is still breathing heavily like the rest of us, although earthly respiration is more often associated with earthquake disaster. I don't know why it's not equated with love, because no matter how the earth moves, it moves.

Yellowstone—established in 1872—is believed to be the first national park on the planet, and certainly the first in the United States. In my mind, it's the equivalent of Eden, which has been closed to mortals since shortly after genesis. How our national park service manages to cram nearly four-million annual visitors into its boundaries without destroying the place is the result of an eternal wrestling match between omnipotence and federal government.

The time of year turned out to be perfect for my visit. Although most of the facilities, including two access roads, had already been closed, nature left plenty to see. I hiked among the Artists Paintpots, listened to Roaring Mountain, and marveled at the veils of steam rising from the shores of Yellowstone Lake. I wasn't alone, especially when I arrived at the infamous Old Faithful Geyser. There, the majority of God's creatures I did meet had two legs.

I toured the park for several days, long enough to learn that when coming upon a clutch of vehicles pulled carelessly off to the shoulder on both sides of the road, it didn't mean there had been a car accident. Instead, it meant genuine wildlife had been sighted, an opportunity for the public to point their Canons and shoot.

The Old Faithful Inn remained true, located just kitty-corner from the old Geezer, but what surprised me was how I caught myself marveling at the gargantuan stone fireplace, the tiered interior balconies railed by skinned and polished tree limbs, and the general rustic Davy Crocket style of the place, as if I'd never seen it before. Clearly, my twelve-year-old brain had been mush, and my memory had rebelled against filing these images away for future reference. I'd become a tourist in my own history.

One other detail I rediscovered involved my first train ride: the Northern Pacific Railway, now served by Amtrak, provided service to Yellowstone in the mid-1960s and my father must have purchased passage on that railway to take his family for a summer vacation. In my brain, something about Yellowstone has always been associated with trains. My visit prompted a very distinct memory of a VistaDome car, where passengers could view a 360-degree panorama of countryside as the train traveled west. I also learned that the railway was first headquartered in Brainerd, Minnesota, the town where I was born. All this information would have been useless to me back then, but now it gushed out of my mental landscape like its namesake, Old Faithful.

I should mention the other fact: catastrophic volcanic eruptions occurred at Yellowstone over two-million years ago, and again 1.2 million years ago, then 600,000 years ago, and once more in the summer of 1965. Geologists will not confirm the last eruption, but that's what I'm saying: the earth moves in subtle ways.

MAYDAY

When I parked beside the locked gate at the forest service's Mayday recreation site, the hefty entrance sign bolted together out of four-by-fours lay flat on the gravel. The green-steel tube where campers are supposed to deposit their fees had turned an autumnal shade of rust. The site insisted the road was closed.

Such a fine campground, decommissioned like so many others, as public land agencies struggle to rein in their spending. I locked the truck before climbing over the gate, just in case the ghosts of former campers had taken to haunting the premises.

Five years ago was the last time I'd stayed overnight at this national forest facility in western Colorado, and I assumed it would always be here, perennial as the grass. Rarely crowded and located only a few miles downstream from the McPhee reservoir dam, this recreational campground served as an ideal fishing corridor, water park, and general pit stop for the contemplation and restoration of the soul. I realize that's a lot to expect from a park, but like much of the public, I depended on our public lands.

This particular spot had a ribbon of concrete that contractors poured beside the river. It still runs nearly the entire length of the campground. At the time of its completion over fifteen years ago, I thought, "Wow, the tax dollars must be as slippery as the fish—strictly catch and release." Now the unnecessary walkway is over-grown with a greenery that doesn't resemble money. Even the massive sandstone wall across the river displays an array of gunshots that pock and mar its surface, but nothing short of a cataclysmic event could decommission this monolithic feature made by nature. It was built by the kind of slow upheaval that bureaucrats will never understand. It requires no budget or maintenance. It's just rock, solid and inspirational.

Every feature I encountered during this comeback tour was on the path to ruin, like those cast iron fire-rings that gaped at me from the dirt and reminded me of burned out stars.

It may seem logical that as our public land budgets are downsized, our accessibility must also be reduced, but logic doesn't originate in the heart. The public may no longer be able to afford Rangers or the regular maintenance of hiking trails, visitor centers, museum displays, bookstores, brochures and trail guides, but if it all has to go, then let it go.

Accessibility, however, should not be on the table, even if there are no tables. Just give us a piece of gravel where we can park and maybe a toilet. We'll provide the toilet paper and enough imagination to appreciate the unimproved natural world. If it's too expensive to maintain the toilets, we'll bare that too.

Nothing is more frustrating than austerity, especially after we've had it all. Of course, nature might disagree. The disaster I surveyed upon arriving at this derelict campground occurred on a glorious afternoon. Everything woody was changing color for fall; wildflowers still speckled the landscape, and the sun poured through the thinly filtered canopy of trees, promising an unusually warm morning and a full-service afternoon, especially for mushrooms sprouting like puffballs.

I know, maybe the "public" isn't sophisticated enough to care for its public lands without some stewardship. Passes, permits, stickers, and policies in place once improved the public's access. But as I circled this overbuilt and now decaying campground, I couldn't help asking myself, "How much of this stuff do we really need?" Show me a trail marker. I might find my own way.

Just like Rip Van Winkle, I wondered, could another unmanaged twenty years make this place more frightening, or more beautiful?

TACKY TOURS

With the eternal threat of lean financial times facing our national parks, and with so many tourists idling at the gates, you might have thought that it's time to consider a few alternative travel itineraries for your summer vacation. After all, peak season was being defined by the National Park Service as the "busiest contiguous five-month period of visitation," which roughly translates into exactly when you have the opportunity to visit them.

Harshly criticized, a proposed new fee structure prompted administrators to rethink their plan, requiring only modest increases at all 117 parks where fees are charged. Many taxpayers believe congress needs to step up and properly fund the parks it created, but expecting another dysfunctional federal budget to resolve decades of neglect is like Scrooge seeing Teddy Rosevelt's ghost-of-national-parks-past, dressed in a Santa

Claus outfit rattling a set of logging chains in the House of Representatives.

Let me assure you, America's Southwest is filled with kitschy caches of cryptic consumerism, ones that park service personnel wouldn't ever dream of mentioning in public. And for good reason. Your children will love these locations, because they are more cool-and-wow inspired than a bunch of breath-taking scenic vistas comprised of hazardous cliff edges, unstable rocks, and indigenous (sometimes poisonous) plants.

Have you ever seen an actual piece of petrified sloth dung? It might not be your first choice, but it's less expensive than getting into the Grand Canyon and it's on display at the Sonoran Desert Museum in Tucson, a turd protected behind a piece of plexiglass so your children won't be able to play with it, all encapsulated within a simulated cave experience that comes with just the ticket price. Only eleven miles away is a twenty-foot tall concrete wine bottle standing beside the Boondocks Lounge. Maybe the kids could climb on it while you go inside, purchase some liquid refreshment, and find an unregulated campsite out in the boondocks.

Here's another idea if you're touring Arizona. Joanne's Gum Gallery Museum near downtown Quartzite displays over 4,000 pieces of gum that have been put aside by Joanne Brunet herself since she was a little girl in the early 1940s. The gum would easily be a world-class attraction had the specimens been masticated and modeled into miniature portrait replicas of famous people, then stuck to a bedpost, but alas, they are all displayed with their original packaging. Still, it's a time capsule of sorts, and the admission is free.

New Mexico has a reputation for its military testing grounds, aliens, and nuclear bombs, but the town of Mesilla contains a reputedly classy dining experience at the Stabbed Lovers Haunted Restaurant. As the story goes, two teenage lovers, a servant girl and the son of a wealthy family, were discovered in a compromising position. The young boy's mother then stabbed the girl with sewing shears but during the tussle she managed to skewer her son, too.

Both "ghost chairs" where the tragic spirits reportedly still sit are off-limits. Don't even think about sitting there.

Home to four of the seventeen popular national parks where fees nearly skyrocketed, Utah still has room for more than a few unusual escapes. The cliff where the movie characters Thelma and Louise took the plunge in Dead Horse Point State Park near Moab is there, and so is an early 1900s bank built entirely from 80,000 bricks that were mailed to Vernal, Utah (not even postage due), but the gem has to be the mounted dog head at the Shooting Star Saloon in Huntsville. Buck—a Guinness Book Record for the World's Largest St. Bernard—weighed in at 298 pounds. The preserved head (possibly drooling, possibly not) hangs on the wall above a special booth in Utah's oldest saloon. The saloon's burgers were once written up in *USA Today* as the third best in America, but in that particular booth they'll always be under a Buck.

If time is as scarce as money, perhaps the Four Corners Monument, situated on tribal land and not under park service jurisdiction, will appeal to you. For just a few dollars paid at the gate, an entire family can buy souvenirs while playing hopscotch in the crosshairs of Colorado, New Mexico, Arizona, and Utah, the only spot in America where visiting four states at virtually the same moment is possible, a kind of transporter beam experience, especially useful when the sun's hot and you've lost the urge to energize.

For a change, it would be nice to hear of an unwavering commitment to national parks from our elected officials without having to rely on a backup plan. While we wait for the impossible, why not purchase an annual pass which gives you access to every national park. Think of it as contributing to the restoration of America's public lands and improving their aging infrastructure—roads, bridges, campgrounds, waterlines, bathrooms, and other visitor services. The task must be an enormous undertaking.

And just in case "enormous" generates the kind of electric excitement your family craves, the world's largest nose can be found in Artvin, Turkey. It comes attached to Mehmet Ozyurek who was born in 1949, and believe it or not, he's still alive. It measures 4.5 inches. You can bet your last vacation dollar that it will cost more than an annual park pass to see that unnatural wonder.

WALKING ON WATER

In the 1952 movie *Viva Zapata*, Marlon Brando portrayed Mexican revolutionary Emiliano Zapata. One of my favorite novelists, John Steinbeck, wrote the screenplay. But instead of reminding you more about the film, let me direct your attention to a completely non-Hollywood experience, an often explored Zapata not crafted by film-folk but by the natural forces of geology and weather which can be viewed by climbing three and a half miles of switchbacks along a rocky road to the trailhead for Zapata Falls. You'll have to bring your own popcorn.

Great Sand Dunes National Park & Preserve, southeast of Alamosa, Colorado, is where you'll have to go. My first visit occurred twenty years ago. At the time, Medano Creek pulsed and surged through the sand like an ocean tide, and I felt its mysterious current pounding against my legs. I still carry that experience, tucked safely into my memory's saddlebags.

This spring I stood there once again, beside the park's thirty-square-mile sandbox, staring at the snow-capped mountains beyond. A few determined hikers with walking sticks were ambitiously trudging toward the highest visible dune peak, even as a stiff wind out of the southwest conscientiously erased their tracks. Children playing at the edge of the creek shouted and splashed in the water. Spring break had blossomed at the best beach in Colorado. I shed my jacket and sat on it like a towel while brushing damp sand from my bare feet.

My thoughts ran back toward the turnoff sign I had passed on my way into the park that pointed toward Zapata Falls. The word drummed a rhythm in my head. *Zapata, Zapata, Zapata.* Like raindrops from some imaginary cloud. A thirty-foot waterfall in this kind of desert? So remarkable a thought that I tied my shoelaces, then glanced toward the parking lot instead of the nearby sandy slopes. My plans for a hike suddenly shifted to a new location. I had to take a look.

The truck climbed three-and-a-half miles of knobby river-rocked access, bucking like a braying mule over a rough road surface. Ten miles per hour, with a few acceleration bursts up to nearly fifteen. The climb felt like it lasted for hours.

When I reached the trailhead a single vehicle was parked there, and the view was spectacular. Below the overlook, the tallest sand dunes in North America stretched out lazily in the shadow of the much taller snowcapped Sangre de Cristo mountains. The information board at the trailhead explained in bold print that to reach the falls a hiker had to exert only a half-mile of effort, but it was all uphill, including a hazardous stumble into the flow of a rushing creek, through a maze of loose, slippery rocks. Basically, it said, count on getting your feet wet. I glanced at my dry boots and thought, well, at least I'm not barefoot anymore.

Trail conditions proved ideal—dry and not too steep. Spring had arrived here before me. Green grass and tiny mountain flowers basked in the sun. I stepped to the side as two young women outfitted in tennis shoes, tights, and camisoles headed back down the trail, distracted by their cell phones, quickly glancing up only to return to the view of the selfies they had collected at the waterfall.

A half-a-mile breezed by. When I reached the nexus where water and trail merged, I found the creek but it had been lulled into a trance, still meditating on winter, still covered with snowpack and ice. Clinging to a rock wall, I carefully inched my way toward the sound of rushing water. I was standing on a frozen platform above the trail while invisible water gushed audibly below my feet. Farther upstream, a slot in the rock grew wider, as if caught in a searchlight, illuminating the sparkling and slippery surface.

Slick rocks towered above me. The notch broadened to scoop out a wide cavern. I slid along the wall to steady myself, using it like a handrail. Suddenly I could see where the top opened to the sky and sunlight played against the surface of a massively layered ice sculpture that had crawled down to the floor where I stood. I could hardly believe it before noticing that within the massive cone of ice a ribbon of water pulsed through it, not over it. The creek was contained like a snake by its winter skin.

The cavern trickled and dripped, trickled and dripped—a space so full of moisture it floated down from the skylight as a flutter of whimsical snowflakes, like in a snow globe, and I was standing at the center of this little universe, stirred, but not shaken.

SEDIMENTAL JOURNEY

The cone-shaped formations at New Mexico's Tent Rock National Monument stand tall, having survived an era of great upheaval. Good for them. As I approached the park entrance gate, I overheard the employee on duty giving phone instructions to an invisible workman about some scheduled repair.

"We may be closed tomorrow," he announced to his hand. "Yeah, I'm kinda hoping for a day off."

While I waited for him to finish his call, I scratched my head, puzzled by the news that the park service would be celebrating a holiday. I had no idea what it might be. I even feared for a moment that I'd become a run-of-the-mill, too-busy-to-pay-attention kind of American. Then it dawned on me. A government shutdown starts tomorrow, if stopgap funding isn't negotiated by midnight.

No one can be blamed for not remembering such an irregular holiday, our national celebration of partisan politics. Instead of the usual flags, why not just refuse to wear Republican red or Democrat blue?

Sadly, the federal employee clad in brown and green standing before me had to show up for work the following day, even though three days earlier he must have listened with interest as the Republican White House drastically reduced the size of two other national monuments, Bears Ears and Grand Staircase-Escalante, both located in Utah, and both designated by Democratic presidents.

This political climate forces a person to grapple with the mind of a border schizophrenic, an advocate for building walls while at the same time knocking national monument boundaries down. I wouldn't blame park service employees if they started calling in every morning just to find out how much their salaries have been down-sized overnight.

Lucky for me, I'd only planned to hike two miles of trail on five thousand acres of safeguarded land. At the time I felt secure, confident that the trail wouldn't be rolled up like a carpet and hauled away before I returned to my truck. There are people who still believe in public trust and I trust them, but the ones who believe the State of New Mexico is in Mexico continue to make me nervous.

Tent Rocks was legally set aside under the 1906 Antiquities Act as a national monument by President Bill Clinton in 1996. It preserves for future generations unique geological sculptures that formed when volcanic eruptions spewed enormous rock fragments and prompted an avalanche of pyroclastic flow. Seven million years later I can only say, cool!

I am not, however, impressed with the partisan effort to shrink our national heritage. If the Bundy family of Nevada ranchers who led an armed revolt against the BLM at two locations in the West, and the armed ATV riders who ripped across the fragile terrain of Puebloan ruins in southeast Utah are leaders in a new era of public awareness, then I'm pinning my hopes for the future on a few more active volcanos. As I hiked the trail, a steep climb through a magnificently carved slot canyon, a flurry of what first looked like volcanic ash began to fall. It turned out to be snow. The idea that I might reach a vista where I could look back on this land motivated me to crawl over many wedged rocks, slipping through crevices so narrow I feared getting stuck.

We could all benefit from a better view. A chance to rise above the bickering and truly see the kind of legacy most Americans hold dear, this patchwork of public lands, national monuments and national parks, that should exist in perpetuity. The extraction of resources is a poor excuse for turning our cultural heritage into tailings.

As I climbed, I realized how fortunate I was to live in the West, able to be present in what others only hear about in the news. To them, a national monument is an abstraction. To me, it's the dirt in my backyard, which could be why I get so sedimental about our public lands.

When I reached the mesa top, I turned around and sat down just to catch my breath. Looking off into the expansive distance, I could see the Sangre de Cristo, Jemez, and Sandia mountains. Snow continued to fall. Over a precipice, I looked down on a congregation of Tent Rock formations standing at attention like soldiers, like old stone spires, like the relics of prehistoric cathedrals.

We may need to temporarily close Washington D.C. Send all our politicians on a little career-related holiday. Democrats to Utah. Republicans to Mexico.

THE DESERT DECEIVES

A sign at New Mexico's Yost Draw trailhead depicts a Bureau of Land Management path that ends at an overlook with a view of the ninety-mile historic route where four hundred years ago "thousands of wagons, people, and livestock migrated between Mexico City and the small New Mexican towns on New Spain's northern frontier."

For me, this sunny morning with a cool March breeze insisted I take a hike, but not that harsh encounter along a rugged landscape with little or no water, firewood, or forage for livestock. Conquistadors named it "Jornado del Muerto," or "Dead Man's Journey." I opted for the BLM's short overlook trail.

My daypack provided hope: a water bottle, a spotting scope, extra sunscreen and plenty of room to stash my flimsy windbreaker as the day warmed. With a sun-hat on my head, I headed out.

Small stones bordered both sides of the path, gradually disappearing as I hiked, replaced by the natural desert rocks scattered randomly on the surrounding terrain. These prompted me to stop, pick one up, appreciate its colors and intrusions, speculate on its geology, then drop it.

According to fitness trainers, a one-and-a-half-mile hike should end up taking under an hour. It took me two, and no hint of hardship explains why. No doubt I spent too much time reading each interpretive plaque along the way, and visiting with my companions, the rocks. A short climb where the trail ended brought me to the overlook and a view of the tedious south-north journey. Despite four centuries of wind, rain, sun and earthly upheaval, visible ruts from wagon wheels are preserved along portions of that track, too far away to clearly see, but the photo at the last interpretive panel stood as proof enough for me.

"Jornado del Muerto," was inspired by the grisly remains of a German trader, Bernado Gruber. Why is beyond me. So much beauty exists in that desert—and every desert. The vistas I encountered continue to inspire me, but not like a gruesome story.

You see, the Spanish Inquisition had crashed into North America's Spanish territories like a riptide in the

1600s. Gruber made his living leading mules and horses packed with trading goods throughout the area. Christmas morning, 1668, after chatting up potential customers before church, he climbed into a choir loft and inscribed +ABNA+ADNA+ on some tiny scraps of paper in his pocket, then whispered to the choir members that eating just one would protect the consumer from harm for twenty-four hours.

Little did he know a nineteen-year-old who'd taken one of the papers would repeat and demonstrate the same claim later that day to some curious Native Americans in a ceremonial kiva. After swallowing it, the boy pretended to stab his hand with an awl, then lifted it—undamaged—for his audience to see. They must have been amazed, and he must have giggled about his trick all the way home until his wife convinced him to report Gruber to the Inquisition.

Gruber was arrested, found guilty of witchcraft, and jailed. Managing an eventual escape with meager supplies on a roan horse, he headed south back over "the desert trail." Spaniards went after him, but he wasn't found until a trading party came upon the remains of his dead horse two years later, "still tied to a tree by its halter," and nearby, a skull and bones, all of them stripped clean by vultures.

I knew nothing about Gruber until weeks after I returned home, but it's clear a desert can be deadly when desperate people undertake such journeys unprepared or rely on hired shysters as guides.

Heading back to the car, I picked up a hefty volcanic stone, ovular in shape like an ostrich egg, all black but banded by a unique tan stripe like a leather belt. Thinking it would remind me of my trek, I decided to take it home, so I put it in my backpack and continued toward the parking lot.

The stone was ponderous, but I had less than a mile to carry it. Only after reaching the car and putting the backpack down did I fully realize I'd lugged a souvenir not only the size of a skull, but it also felt as heavy as a few cool, clear gallons of water. In the desert water always acquires more weight.

5: And Eavesdrop on the Natural World

AN ODIOUS TO SPRING

For many people, the March equinox serves as a traditional marker, but not for me. It's when the irrigation water starts gurgling and flowing that spring has officially arrived in Montezuma County, as far as I'm concerned. Before the Montezuma Valley Irrigation Company releases its flood, I'm always a bit frantic, like Noah trying to hammer together an Ark in preparation for an appointed day.

The pond needs scouring, ditches require burning, all the hoses untangled, pipe arranged, and the pumps nudged from hibernation, installed and primed, all while the tiller and the lawnmower wait in the wings like understudies to this great seasonal drama. The winter relaxes me, but then the spring rebukes me for being lazy.

To be fair, I should mention how the irrigation water got here in the first place. In 1886, the first ambitious Montezuma Valley irrigation project settled in for the long haul, its goal to move Dolores River water through a tunnel to what the company hoped would become an irrigated Eden. It took three years to complete the work, and the company went bust. I sympathize. My experience 130 years later trying to get my shares of water to properly irrigate my patch of ground confirms that water moves along an altogether different path than money.

I'm sure the crocuses don't get as crazy as I do. They poke their nubile nubs up through the dirt while the sun is beating down and they prepare to stretch, like tiny yawns along the flower bed, all of them beautiful and equipped for nothing more industrious than encouraging a few insects to crawl inside their blossoms and tickle them. I hate that about the crocuses.

I'm also losing a lot of respect for globe willows. Their iconic spherical shape is attributed to their self-pruning quality, which from a distance looks attractive, but it's the wind that does the pruning, not the tree, and every furious spring that blows through the southwest dumps enough kindling on my lawn to start a bonfire. It's just an endless game of pick-up-sticks, dead branches falling through the canopy, littering the lawn. I keep chopping them up and hauling them off, but the gusts start again and I swear the wind starts to sound like a snicker.

On a clear afternoon when the wind isn't blowing, the temperature can climb to seventy degrees. A week of this unseasonal warmth is great for sweeping the porch, picking up dead willow branches, and assessing what else needs to be done, but the lilacs and the forsythia and the apricots and the plums all think it's time to get busy, so they produce their little buds like goosebumps along their branches. Then, an overnight temperature of fifteen degrees freeze-dries their hopes. I haven't seen the lilacs in my yard bloom in the eight years I've lived here. Oh yeah, one year I ate a plum that must have survived like Superman in his Fortress of Solitude. It wasn't exactly sweet, but I savored the pucker.

And what would spring in the Four Corners be without the odor of the newly revived and easily excitable skunks? Three-quarters of a mile from my home, traffic squashes one and the odor of its demise wafts through the neighborhood, settling inside my house. Something about my high ceilings and poor ventilation embraces the smell, like a well-used pair of shoes that retain the stink long after the owner has washed his feet and moved on. There. I think I've touched on four of the five senses: the sound of the water, the pretty-as-a-picture flowers, the frigid, bone-chilling overnight temps, and the smell of skunks. I should say something about taste.

For three weeks, I worked like a brush hog rooting a path along my fence line, cutting through red willows that annually create an impenetrable barrier. I snipped and whipped each stalk out of the way with my lopper, hoping to expose a path to cradle 300 feet of PVC in an old flume that once served as a wooden culvert. The integrity of the structure is still remarkably functional after over seventy years. Every day, the wind blew but, sheltered by thicket, I hardly felt it. I heard only the willows rustling like a box of matchsticks. Each time I stepped into the open to dump another bundle I'd cut, the wind blasted me with dust. The dust stuck to my sweat, powdering my face.

So here's a nod to the fifth sense: everyone who lives in the American Southwest knows the taste of spring.

AMERICAN BIRD

A wild turkey crossed my path last year while I hiked along Petroglyph Trail, a recreational sidebar within the greater Mesa Verde National Park, on Thanksgiving Day, of all days. It posed in the open for an instant and tried to stare me down before calmly moving off—an alert, fully plumed and magnificent specimen of a game bird. I felt as if the bird had stopped to emphasize the difference between itself and the pale, plucked, over-greased variety of America we stuff into so many tiny 350-degree tanning booths on the fourth Thursday each November.

In all fairness to the wild bird, let me mention how Benjamin Franklin confided to his daughter in a 1784 letter that the turkey would have been a better choice for the Great Seal of this country than the bald eagle, which had been officially adopted as our national bird by Congress in 1782. The eagle, he suggested, was a coward, a bird of inferior moral character, a lazy opportunist that scavenged and did not garner its living honestly.

I doubt if Franklin ever weighed the merits of each bird when it came to filling out the Thanksgiving table.

Perhaps I should be at home like so much of America, crowded into one room, partying with friends, watching at least one football game on at least one television, eating a second piece of pumpkin pie, sipping another beer, instead of hiking this silent path. I'll probably get in trouble for saying this, but holidays often prompt an irresistible anti-social feeling inside me, an urge to get off on my own, to participate in no gathering, to share no experiences, to converse almost exclusively with the rocks and trees.

And here I'd arrived at a spot where five hundred years prior to Franklin's familial letter, some anonymous hands with pointy rock tools pecked an array of images into this southwestern Colorado cliff wall, and several of the petroglyphs depicted birds. Maybe they are turkeys, it's hard to tell, but they stand silently posed like the outline of a flattened, open human hand—the same figure all first graders are taught to draw in class before the fall holiday by tracing a line around the peninsulas of their tiny fingers. I counted exactly two birds made of single handprints on the rock wall, and it struck me as a shoo-in for a new adage that a bird of the hand is worth two on the rock.

Eventually I continued along the trail, returning to the Spruce Tree museum, where I paused at that great vantage point overlooking prehistoric cliff dwellings below. The path was still deserted. Turkeys, one; tourists, zero.

Even more than two million years ago, wild turkeys existed, based on the scientific dating of fossil remains, and it's even possible the Aztecs had domesticated a variety of the bird. The turkey was here in North America when the Puritans landed and was still here when Benjamin Franklin flew his kite.

I try to imagine the sheer absurdity of proposals being swatted back and forth by our early politicians that finally concluded in the Great Seal decision, which might have threatened to become our first legislative gridlock, and we should be glad an albatross didn't end up as the emblem for our democracy.

But what troubles me most is that Big Bird has been dragged into the melee during some recent toxic political discourse. Here is a purely American symbol of kindness, stature, and diplomacy—not red, not blue, but yellow. Maybe it's about time this new bird received a nomination for its place on the Great Seal of our country, not predator or prey, not rich or poor, not Republican or Democrat, but an eight-foot pillar of unruffled Big Bird feathers that stands, literally, for rising above it all.

BEAR NECESSITIES

The reported buzz of bear sightings from summer and fall has diminished to a scarcely audible snore since the weather has turned colder. We've all grown a little sleepy hearing the news stories related to sightings and the danger that bears pose to human habitation. I guess we've been living in an updated version of *Goldilocks and the Three Bears*, one where we stay at home while the bears do the breaking and entering.

For many people, the behavior of bears goes barely observed in the natural world, and that is the way it should be. But when a bear shows up on the sundeck of a half-million-dollar home, or worse, takes a few steps through your patio doors to see what's cooking, that's when people usually take a keener interest in what the animal might do. Surely, the bear belongs in the woods and we belong, well, I guess we belong anywhere we decide to carve a six-bedroom, four-and-a-half bath cave out of the wilderness.

Because most of the bears bedded down are dreaming in their dark, cozy caves about berries or maybe, in a few cases, chocolate mousse, I think now is as good a time as any to offer some alternative advice on safely living with bears. I know trained biologists spend their lives out there in the field trying to understand how bears behave, and I want to encourage them to continue. The ideas that follow are strictly mine, inspired by years of experience with human beings. As for bears, all I know for sure is what I read in the newspapers.

According to the news, the Boulder County Nature Association asked that its county commissioners approve a law requiring tickets be issued to those who attract or feed bears. It claims ticketing would be good policy for reducing human-bear contacts, but I'm not so sure. You see, the ticketing would only occur after the fact—after the bear has already made contact. And the problem with bears is that like most human beings, they pick up bad habits quickly.

Once human contact is established, the animal will likely return to its host. As for its host, Colorado state wildlife law currently requires officials to relocate a troublesome bear after its first offense. Then, if the bear returns, officials have the authority to shoot the bear, if they deem it necessary. You've seen the signs in campgrounds hanging like a surgeon general's warning on a pack of cigarettes: A FED BEAR IS A DEAD BEAR. I would gladly go along with the Boulder association's ticketing proposal if it would also embrace the spirit of the Colorado law, that individuals found guilty of attracting or feeding bears should, indeed, be given a ticket; but if the bear returns, I think the matter ought to remain open as to which of the mammals should be shot.

Another danger arises from a bear's instinct to protect its young, at all costs. The instinct seems entirely admirable, and I see a version of the same impulse forwarded in human culture by those who subscribe to the aims of our "Children First" campaign. Still, to a lone hiker in the woods who comes unexpectedly upon a sow and her cubs, the campaign's mission statement sounds hollow. I would, therefore, never go hiking in the woods without children, and since I have no children, then it would be wise to borrow some.

Faced with the massive weight of maternal imperatives along any narrow path in the mountains, both bear and human might simply stare at each other before crashing through the undergrowth in opposite directions, without contact or incident. But if the bear still decides to attack, well then, for the human adult, what an advantage it is to be an advocate of Children First.

Bears might also prove more flexible than human beings, which could account for their increased activity within the boundaries of our habitation. One story can serve as illustration. At Devils Postpile National Monument, a twelve-passenger university van parked in a designated picnic area and a group of biology interns disembarked so they could consume lunch. When one of the interns turned, she saw a bear ambling toward their van. The bear gracefully stuck its head and front paws through a twelve-inch opening left by one of the partially closed windows and pulled itself, fully, into the van. The intern was astonished. She thought that as the bear reached through the window, it would simply yank the entire door off the van, but no. Over 250 pounds of bear managed to squeeze between that narrow opening, locate a single bag of potato chips, and exit the van with the chips in tow.

During this snack attack, someone ran to contact a wildlife official who arrived in time to stand with the rest of the group watching the bear leave the vehicle. He could do nothing, as he explained, because the bear acted on national park land and he only had jurisdiction over state holdings. Ah, for the safety afforded by paperwork.

And speaking of paperwork, everybody remembers the old question: does a bear shit in the woods? Since the beginning of time, the answer has been an obvious yes, except for those who find bear scat on the linoleum beside their refrigerator. Now is perhaps the right time to ask a new question: why would a bear shit in the woods after the park service has provided such nice toilets?

TRASH TREES AND NIGHT VISITORS

In the middle of the night, I woke to the sound of snickering outside my bedroom window. I lay still, ransacking my brain for who might be about to play a trick on me, although I had a good idea who one of the culprits might be.

I reached for my flashlight and slipped out of bed. With one hand, I yanked the curtain aside and with the other I flipped on the switch. The beam caught the glittering eyes of two intruders staring back at me.

Raccoons in my Russian olive tree. In that sweet spot where the greatest limbs converged about five feet off the ground, I habitually find a mound of feces. It accumulates until I decide to blast it loose with the garden hose, always careful to stand clear of the splatter. This has been going on for quite some time, although I had never until this night caught the raccoons in the act.

It's a giant tree, maybe fifty-years old, spreading a canopy of branches over my front yard, and I'm not guilty of planting it. When I stand back to look at it I sigh, because the Russian olive is considered a trash tree, an invasive species that along with the tamarisk, thrives beside riparian corridors and is slated for extermination in many regions of the West.

This particular tree, however, is a stunning example of good deciduous looks. How it survived for half a century in what has become my front yard is beyond me. Its roots must be stealing water from my neighbor's cow pond.

In late summer when the tree is laden with olives, the limbs come alive, bouncing to a bird rhythm as squadrons land in the branches in order to rip the ripe fruit loose. The lawn suffers, littered with the residue of their enthusiasm, from olives that fall to bird poop that whitewashes the nearby fence posts and spatters the lilac leaves.

The olives themselves are pitiful specimens, a misnomer for what we normally think of as companions to a dry martini. Mine are about the size of lima beans, with hard seed casings and tasting as bitter as turpentine, but the tree has found its niche. Once established,

Russian olives can eke out a living nearly anywhere in the arid West.

Squirrels gather and store the seeds. Birds—and especially blackbirds—devour them, although the experts claim there is little evidence to support the conclusion that multiple bird species depend on the fruit. This is hardly the makings of an endangered anything, and I don't think the tree's status will be reevaluated if I add to the scientific record that raccoons eat the olives too, a wildlife fact for which I have irrefutable poop.

If the Russian olive weren't so aggressive—crowding out the cottonwoods, willows, and other so-called native vegetation and sometimes even obstructing our irrigation ditches—it might be cultivated for its benefits. In fact, when it was imported to this country in the early 1900s, ranchers used the tree to curb erosion, deploying it as a windbreak in every wide-open space that needed protection. So much for the wrongheaded notions of the past. Now I keep one tree standing as a year-round habitat toilet. I can't think of any other way to justify its existence to those who would have it down.

Of course, I can't think of any reason for most of the improbable metropolitan drainages like Los Angeles, Phoenix, or Las Vegas to exist in such a barren and inhospitable climate as the West, but sure enough, they do. And they thrive, just like the Russian olive. Roads like tree roots supply the core with nutrients. The municipalities and their utilities grow thicker and tap into the water supplies, damming and diverting that precious liquid we require to produce everything from hay to grapes.

The process repeats itself as our edifices choke out much of the natural vegetation, and civilization emerges to shape its own little monument. So as not to gloss over the obvious, let me just say this: not everything that comes out of us is a marvel to look at.

History is digestion. All of the silvery leaves of my Russian olive eventually yellow and are long-scattered, but for the visiting raccoons, at night this trashy tree contains more than enough privacy. I just wish they'd keep their voices down.

UNREPORTED

It wasn't my fault, but that's not an explanation. A car coming from the other direction pulled to the shoulder a short distance beyond the scene. The driver must have witnessed the collision and was probably as surprised as me, but she wasn't getting out of her vehicle and neither was I. Who has the time or motivation to certify in first-aid training when it comes to resuscitating a three-hundred-pound brown bear?

I should start at the beginning, although it happened so quickly I hardly remember if there was a beginning. My pickup was traveling about fifty miles an hour along the gentle curves that Colorado Highway 62 carves out of the mountains on its way up Dallas Divide. The highway on the Placerville side of the summit is a two-laner, with towering rock walls to my left and a steep descending embankment to my right. A creek rushes through the crease, well below the highway, but much of it is obscured by the lush mountain flora.

The blur that crested the embankment and into my path was hardly recognizable at the moment of its appearance. I tugged the steering wheel toward the centerline to avoid it, but the car coming from the other direction narrowed my options. The brown bear, charging up the embankment like a fur-encrusted meteor, struck my truck on the passenger side, just behind my headlight. Thump. Another thump against the passenger door panel. Then it was over. That quickly. Less than a thought. Barely a paragraph.

The number of animals we dispatch on our highways must be phenomenal. By one estimate, a million lives a day, including birds, mice, squirrels, snakes, rabbits, prairie dogs, gophers, skunks, raccoons, turtles, frogs, cats, and dogs. We call them roadkill, not fatalities. The bigger the dead critters are however—like deer, elk, and bear—make us sit up and pay attention.

My bear remained motionless, dead still I thought, until I watched her head rise from the road surface and twist, a bit like a periscope, looking around. Then she made a valiant attempt to stand, rose on all fours until a front leg buckled and she collapsed again into a heap. She moved as if she'd been drinking, weaving and wobbling, a fifty mile an hour highball altering her brain.

A few inert seconds passed that seemed to take full minutes before she made another attempt to stand. I'm watching like a gawker at this scene of misfortune. I'm thrilled that she's moving. I'm horrified to watch her struggle. I want to get out of the truck and help. I don't want to get out of the truck and help. I'm a wreck, literally and figuratively. Then she puts all her bear-like prerogatives into their proper perspectives, stands, twists, and before I can say, "Holy Bear Shit!" she lunges off the road, back down the embankment from which she first came.

She survived! I still can't believe it. What a rugged piece of fur and flesh. I climbed out of the truck and cautiously approached the shoulder, peered into the natural abyss at the side of the road. No sign of a bear, just the sound of a rushing creek. I shouted, "Sorry!" but I had the feeling forgiveness is just a human sentiment, an indulgence we rely on for the assurance of salvation.

The car that had pulled over to observe my drama started its engine and drove away. There was no blood on the pavement. I turned back to my truck to inspect the damage and see if I could leave the scene. In addition to the crumpled panels, a chunk of plastic near the headlight had been sprung like a flag. I knew the wind would tear it loose, so I found a roll of black electrical tape in my tool bag and fastened it. The tire had plenty of room to roll inside its wheel well. I could drive, and with a Wallflowers CD playing I could make it home with one headlight.

The next day I took the truck to a body shop for an estimate. The manager concluded it would cost over $4,000, and it would take eight or ten days to make the repairs. I'd chosen to drive with a $500 deductible. Ah, I thought, when it comes to suffering, we make ourselves into the best victims.

I do wish the bear a long life, but if she woke in the morning with a throbbing headache I wouldn't be surprised.

PAPERBACK RIDER

I was sitting in a comfortable chair one evening, reading a vintage western, when I glanced out the window to see a horse cropping the grass along my driveway. I don't own a horse. I don't want a horse. Too many neighbors breed horses only to stand them like silhouettes against the horizon.

I went out to the porch for a better look, thinking I'd encounter a part-time cowboy. I called out to the empty horizon: Yoo-hoo? Nothing but a nicker from the horse.

Acres of print examine the plight of wild horses in the West, often referred to as "mustangs," and I'm not suggesting the problem deserves any less attention. Finicky horse advocates will argue that the term "wild mustangs" is erroneous; such horses aren't wild, just feral, having been introduced by the Spanish centuries ago from their own domesticated stock.

But whether these horses fairly or unfairly compete for forage on public grazing lands or whether they are a native or invasive species is beside the point. The horse in my driveway had a ribcage as distinct as a xylophone and she was not wild, just worn out.

She politely glanced up, allowed me to approach, then went on cropping the grass. As I ran my hand along her neck and flanks, it became obvious my guest hadn't just missed a meal or two. She'd been systematically ignored until her mere presence must have chided her owners into turning her loose.

Wild horses may be scattered all across the West, but it's the domestic stock being "set free" to find their destinies that worries me. Horse owners down on their economic luck think they'll save bales of cash by letting their charges wander. The notion that horses like feral dogs and cats will find their own way is absurd, even for dogs and cats.

In the literature children are fed, the image of equine *hug-ability* is just too precious. *Black Beauty* and *My Friend Flicka*, to name a few, are stories that tug at the heartstrings, prompting children to stroke a plastic replica of a dream they hope to transform one day into flesh. I don't know how many youngsters receive ponies for their birthdays, but based on my own informal gallop poll, it's grownups all across the West who are not able to rein in their urge to own a horse.

In Alice Walker's book, *Horses Make A Landscape Look More Beautiful,* these are not the same ones strung for miles along our rural fence lines, pulling up the grass by the roots until paradise is reduced to an acre of bare dirt.

I found a plastic pail in the garage and dumped in some oatmeal, then pulled a rope off a nail. One taste of oats and my mystery horse followed me anywhere. I followed the trail of horse apples along the road, all the way up to the highway and back again. Every neighbor's horse rushed across its allotted pasture to shinny up to the wire, whinny and snort, as if gossiping about this stranger. We ended up back in my driveway, which is a poor excuse for a horse refuge, because my property is not fenced, but I have a good-fences-make-good-neighbors neighbor who once visited my property to collect his truant bull. We get quite a parade of wandering livestock across our land for the simple reason that we don't fence them out.

He said no, it wasn't his horse but offered to put her up in a small pasture where he'd quartered three of another neighbor's horses to clean up his grass. A sort of weed and feed negotiation.

As he worked at undoing the gate chain, I removed the rope from around my horse's neck. I say "my horse" but really she wasn't anyone's horse, not any more. She leaned her long head against my shoulder and held it there for a ponderous moment before I urged her into the company of strangers.

Later, I found a man who provides rescue services for animals, but he had no room for a horse and suggested I check with the brand inspector, which sounded like a great idea until I learned the horse would likely end up at the sale barn, which meant horse meat, not adoption.

One evening, as I returned from town I noticed all of my neighbor's horses were gone. I thought about stopping, about asking, but the way the plot works out in so many traditional westerns, the horse heads into the sunset. And now, instead of a horse, I'm saddled with this memory.

FEATHERED APPARITIONS

While my neighbors were absent, I kept an eye on their house to make sure things stayed safe. Not so much a neighborhood watch as a casual glance in their direction whenever I happened to walk past. I didn't know if they had any kind of alarm system installed, but I stayed far enough away to make sure I didn't find out.

One morning, I heard an unusual ruckus coming from next door. For such a quiet neighborhood, the noise immediately caught my attention. At first I thought it sounded human, but then I recognized the sound: the honky-horn-blowing commotion Canada geese make when passing overhead. What troubled me was that the noise didn't melt into thin air as one expects. The geese, it seemed, were circling overhead in a holding pattern instead of driving their wedge toward a distant horizon.

Stepping outside for a peek, I couldn't believe what I saw. On the roof of my neighbor's two-story house, pacing the shingles like sentries, four flat-footed geese stopped and stared at me while a dozen or more of their companions grazed the brown lawn below. The sight unnerved me, as if a squad of goose-stepping guards had taken over. I waved my arms and shouted, hoping to shoo them away. They stayed, stolid and alert, perhaps even reporting my behavior to their supervisors. I had been dismissed, so I returned to my house.

In our community, seeing geese is not unusual. They settle in our parks, poop on our sidewalks, and would, if they could swing a club, play golf on the many acres of our irrigated fairways. Once a migratory species, many Canada geese have found urban and suburban areas provide a comfortable living without the bother of flying thousands of miles. These days, if I'm flying, I'm lucky to be handed a tiny bag of pretzels.

Eventually the "goostapo" moved off, but I still wondered about the ones that chose to spend their feeding time on my neighbors' roof. Had living in our developed world skewed their natural instincts so badly they yearned to find new perches? Or is it porches? Divided from their natural instincts, it's hard to say what motivates a goose to behave in a non-goose way.

Once while walking past the city park, I stopped to watch a group of about six people plus two police officers pursue a goose back and forth across the lawn. For more than fifteen minutes, the goose evaded the trap: a man holding out an old blanket like a matador. The idea was that he would throw a net over the bird if the silly thing ever got close enough. I joined in the chase and later heard that the goose had repeatedly tried to bite a child, which prompted a call to the police, which led to the all-out pursuit, which eventually resulted in its capture. It was as wild a goose chase as I'd ever seen.

A few domesticated geese have endeared themselves to their owners, but the birds aren't typically known for being cuddly or affectionate. Goslings like all babies are adorable but try to get near one—even when the parents seem to be temporarily distracted—and you'll experience a goose's dark side. Males especially are noted for being aggressive. In one documented case, a goose killed another goose by persistently driving its head into the mud, resulting in the victim's death by suffocation. It's no wonder I can't help thinking of my neighbor's roof geese as a viable product line for an organic home-security system.

I still don't have an answer for their unorthodox roof behavior, but I have settled on a pet theory. Because I walk past the house regularly, I've reflected on that singular event so obsessively that a reasonable explanation has finally emerged. The goose photos I took may have distracted me from noticing the one detail that inspired my "ah ha" moment.

The neighbors recently installed an array of solar panels along the southern exposure of their roof. While it proved to be a wise investment electrically and ecologically, it may have added a layer of complexity and confusion from a bird's perspective.

Gliding along with the wind under his wings, glancing down, attentive to every sparkle of water where a lush marsh or pond might provide a nice post-flight snack, the goose flying point feels responsible for the squadron trailing along. *There!* He sees a ripple of reflected light. All the flap behind him convinces him it's break time. He trims his wing angle and prepares for the descent.

Science may not back me up on this. Ornithologists could be snickering up their sleeves, dismissing my observations as just another amateur bird-brained theory. We'll never know for sure, because the evolution of geese has not yet bridged our interspecies communication gap, and I felt stupid ordering those geese to get down. It was the down, after all, that helped get them up there in the first place.

SHOOTING THE BREEZE

It's a beautiful autumn day, the mountain trail cobbled with golden leaves like a path to heaven. The sun warms your back, a breeze chatters among the leaves. You're listening intently to the conversation when the crack of two rifle shots pierces the air. You're not the target, but the sound startles you, those bullets speeding along undisclosed trajectories of your imagination.

Moments like these remind me that autumn in the high country is unavoidably hunting season, when our multi-use federal lands sport camo-and-orange attire. The expression "to die for" may or may not apply in this case.

A friend of mine related his experience bowhunting this year. He "filled" his tag on his first day out, and said he had a good trip but felt disappointed. What would he do with the rest of the season? For safety's sake, I suggested cleaning his bow.

The good news? Hunting-related accidents have dramatically declined in the last decade to about eighty or ninety annual fatalities nationwide. My chance of being killed by drowning, car crash, terrorism, or the kind of poor judgment that leads to so many unforeseen deaths is far greater than being unintentionally shot while hiking. Hunters are not the problem. So, why doesn't my brain just relax and take a hike?

It's no mystery that I am not a hunter, as if you couldn't guess. The meat that I harvest comes from the deli, and for me a good hunting trip occurs when there's a sale and I arrive early on the first day.

My father tried teaching me to hunt. We marched through the dry cornfields in rural Minnesota like soldiers, me assigned to my row with a half-dozen or so empty rows between us, trying to flush a plump pheasant out of hiding. I never killed one, and although I heard the occasional report of my father's shotgun, I don't remember us ever returning home with a bird. He issued me his old single shot, bolt-action 22, apparently reluctant to buy an additional shotgun until I perfected my skills, a reasonable strategy for protecting himself from me.

But we did have some luck, the kind I reminisce about these days as the good kind, a male bonding ritual of sorts without the killing, a rite of passage without the one-upmanship. As the day unraveled and our shadows lengthened, we behaved more like two hikers absent-mindedly carrying firearms, out for a walk in the countryside.

My fondest memory from our hunting trips involves setting up cans on a stump or fallen log and practicing knocking them down like tin targets at a carnival booth. My father became genuinely excited when I hit one, the flush of pride visible in his cheeks, the praise and camaraderie bubbling from within. He'd served as an infantryman in World War II and had plenty of shooting experience, but he refused to talk about the killing part despite my earnest and persistent questions. What I learned during our cornfield boot camp was to stop asking, because when I did ask he simply changed the subject, closed himself up, and returned to his drill-sergeant self. What I grew to love most involved simply being outdoors, the sound of the crackling leaves and cornstalks as I tested my stealth. The sun, the wind, the crisp cold air when we first stepped out of the car. I didn't want to actually shoot a pheasant, but I sometimes wished one would conveniently fall from the sky so I could run over, pick it up, and ask my father, "Is this what you want from me?"

We'd tramped the cornfields until a late hour one particular afternoon, finally deciding to call it quits. At the edge of a field where a few trees provided some shade, we trudged to a standstill, listening, not saying a word while the world inhaled its collective breath. Making sure my safety was engaged, I lowered the butt of my rifle to rest beside my boot. At that same instant, a pheasant flushed from the tall grass between us, so close one of us might have reached and snatched it from the air. I thought my brain or my heart had exploded. Or simply that I'd just been shot. Normally a pheasant prefers to run, but if startled it can burst upwards at great speed, wings thrumming a blur.

My desire to hunt vanished as completely as that bird. Coulda, shoulda, woulda mighta been our conversation on the way home, but for me the heart has always known what to say before the brain can rationalize an explanation. It's like a sixth sense, knowing when to call it a day.

STUNK WITHOUT A SOUND

We'd gone to bed, blithely unaware that our property was being cased. You'd think we would have heard something but we're normally deep sleepers, especially when the summer's hot and a cool breeze finally works its way through an open window. I assume the culprit wore black, like most of them do, and I also suspect it made little difference whether we were or were not at home. We slept right through it.

The next morning it was clear we'd been hit. The house stunk, an odor no one mistakes. With my head under the pillow, I sang a muffled version of that line from Laudon Wainwright's golden oldie, "Dead skunk in the middle of the road, stinking to high heaven. Then I jumped out of bed, opening every window and door, knowing that it would probably get worse before it got better. It got worse. The odor invaded the entire house, as if the white stripe of morning had landed squarely on

the back of the night and we were living under its great bel
ly.

I can officially report there's little reliable information about how to successfully eliminate skunk odors,
especially if you rely on your neighbors. What I heard
recounted as sure-fire methods sounded worth trying,
although you have to remember that I was desperate.
For example, a lady informed me if you wash a dog
with tomato juice (and just a dash of Worcester sauce)
it will remove a skunk's odor. Unfortunately, I don't
own a dog, and it would have been silly to wash the
entire house in tomato juice. I did the next best thing. I
thanked her and went back to my stinky house. Then,
I poured myself a glass of tomato juice, added some
vodka, and hoped the remedy would at least stop the
smell from rotting my insides.

Outside the house, I could tell that the strongest odor
originated near the front porch. I hooked up the hose
and did my own spraying. I figured the best remedy had
to be the hair of the skunk that hit you.

But the odor wouldn't go away. When we closed the
house, it smelled as if the skunk was trapped inside. If we
opened the doors, the odor wafted through. I suspected
the skunk had taken up residence, perhaps underneath,
in a space which I have nightmares about inspecting.

By far the most popular answer to the question, "How do you get rid of a skunk?" was to shoot it. But you can't shoot what you can't see, and even if I owned military infrared goggles and odor seeking bullets, I'm a terrible killer. A local farmer's supply store offered to sell me a live trap, but they weren't too keen on taking the trap back once I got it filled.

Then, someone suggested mothballs—someone whose face I can't remember, and I wish I could, because I still have two pounds of mothballs I'd like to give away. According to my source, skunks can't tolerate the smell of mothballs. So I purchased an economy-sized box and instead of crawling under the trailer, I opened the access hatch and tossed handful after handful of mothballs in every conceivable direction. As it turned out, humans can't tolerate the smell of mothballs either. For two days I fluttered around the house like a moth trapped in my grandmother's attic. I couldn't decide which was worse, the skunk or the mothballs. Finally, we couldn't stand it and I crawled under the trailer with a flashlight to gather each mothball and place it in a Ziplock bag—a kind of toxic Easter egg hunt, with an elusive skunk for a bunny. Now we live in a house with only a subtle, blended odor of...dare I say it?... skunk-balls. The idea of fusion at its worst. Naturally, we sleep in the camping trailer parked in the driveway. The air is getting better, really. And if you have any other suggestions, please keep them to yourself.

WHAT THE LIZARD KNOWS

By the first week in October, the aspens start igniting like candles and the scrub oak begins to rust. I'm burning a tank of precious gas, taking a color tour of the high country, our most transitory art gallery here in the Southwest. No more than a fortnight, give or take a few days, to catch the best of the show. Sub-zero nights, temperate days, followed by sudden wind gusts will strip the stands of trees bare with little warning.

Even before I reach Rico while driving up Highway 145, I've counted at least a half dozen vehicles pulled off the pavement, cameras at the ready, sucking the scenery in and loading it onto their digital flatbeds. If color were audible, it would sound like a Fourth of July crowd, the *oohs* and *aahs* deployed like airbags inside every car, drivers leaning into the next curve, and the next one, and the next. Every passenger transformed into a hunting dog, pointing. And every dog disgusted that it has to compete for a chance to get its own head out the window.

At 10,000, feet elevation, it takes until mid-July for summer to fully arrive. Up where Lizard Head Peak casts its shadow, spring appears late, and autumn shows up early. My camping thermometer registered thirty-two degrees on June fourth and thirty-two degrees again on August 14th. If summer can squeeze between these seasonal markers, it may only last a month, but what a glorious season.

If the lizard's head pokes skyward at 10,000 feet, then its tail must reach all the way down to the town of Cortez, where I begin my color tour each autumn. In thirty years, I have run up and down the lizard's spine countless times, or at least enough to know I should stop counting.

According to experts, the fall colors we see are actually present in the leaves when they first appear in the spring, but the abundance of water in the soil sends the trees into a kind of chlorophyll overload, overpowering the yellows, oranges, reds, and purples. Green is what we get, all spring and summer, which is fine with me, as long as the green is accompanied by warmer blue skies. As the chlorophyll in the leaves catches sun and uses the light for energy, it changes water from the ground and carbon dioxide from the air into glucose. Green: just another case of sugar addiction.

If you prefer a magical explanation, then imagine giant chameleons inhabiting the rocks, their skin scaled over with leaves, stretching out in the sun, many of them larger than Bigfoot, or Nellie, or even King Kong. With about 160 species of chameleons accounted for, there's no reason why they wouldn't come in a range of colors, including pink, blue, red, orange, turquoise, yellow, and green. When the weather gets cold, of course, they migrate to warmer climes like the snowbirds.

In the end, it really doesn't matter why the leaves change, only that they do, every year, with ample time for people to catch them on a weekend drive, at a relaxed pace, not just sneaking a peek through the windshield while commuting between some overly familiar rock and an equally hard place.

During my first autumn in Colorado, an elderly secretary I'd met waylaid me in the school district office on a Friday afternoon, demanding me to be ready for a drive into the mountains on Saturday morning. At eight a.m., she said, and she'd pick me up at the door.

"Where are we going?"

"We're off to see the Lizard."

"May I bring my best friend?"

"Only if her name isn't Toto."

"What sort of gear should I pack?"

"Jackets and your rose-colored glasses."

She arrived promptly at eight and didn't even shut off her engine. Pam and I climbed in, exchanged greetings, and our driver's foot was against the gas pedal before we could buckle up.

In the back of her little Subaru hatchback, she'd stowed a picnic blanket, a wide-mouthed thermos of homemade chili, water bottles, and a pint of peppermint schnapps. Her yellow-brick road looped from Cortez to Telluride to Ouray to Silverton to Durango and back to Cortez. The three of us pulled over and laughed frequently along the way, one of those memories that sets up like concrete and remains solid enough for a lifetime of driving. Then, she deposited us at our doorstep just as the setting sun tried to imitate the panoply of leaves.

Since then my rose-colored glasses have been useless.

6: Before Checking Your Inheritance

STAR POWER

"It's not in the stars to hold our destiny but in ourselves." —William Shakespeare

While shopping just after the holidays for discounted Christmas items, I overheard a conversation between a customer and a cashier. I should have moved along and minded my own business, but I was intrigued when the employee started gushing about her children's thoughtfulness. They'd bought her a star for Christmas.

In my mind, I pictured an elegant ornament for the top of her tree, maybe illuminated by LED sparkles, or even a hand-crafted piece of glass. Something to replace a worn-out angel. I could get excited about a well-done star.

Lingering near the gift-card display, eavesdropping, I learned that the star was not anything as trivial as a holiday keepsake. The woman meant an actual star, one of those "billions and billions" of heavenly bodies that Carl Sagan raved about. This cashier's star was apparently located somewhere along, or below, Orion's belt.

My first reaction: who in the world would pay good earth-bound money for a piece of the heavens that (so far) nobody owns? Apparently, the cashier's children. My second reaction: those poor children must have been shamelessly scammed.

When I returned home I searched the internet and discovered at least one portal for stellar gift-giving. At Online Star Register (OSR) anyone with $33 can name a star for themselves or for a loved one. But for a mere $54, customers can opt for the "gift pack," which includes free shipping! I'm not sure if that results in a chunk of space debris streaking across the sky, heading straight for your residential coordinates, or just the possibility that a little stardust might be slipped into your mailbox.

The Netherlands-based company has been selling stars "since the start of this millennium." A sampling of previously registered names include Caterina, Matt Barrett, Chico, and Deb. Sophias Grace is on the register too—without an apostrophe—but perhaps the grammatical error is for emphasis, a subtle suggestion that the namesake better not even think about taking possession.

Alright, enough speculation, because I'm fairly certain the vast majority of OSR's customers are sincere in their desire to bestow a unique tribute for their loved ones.

Love itself is often difficult to express. That it exists and grows brighter with familiarity and vigilance is a characteristic of a star, and that it can fade and burn itself out long before we notice it's gone, sadly, also typifies such celestial bodies. Any heart seeking to underscore its love shouldn't be faulted for trying.

But I'm troubled by the nineteenth-century mentality of manifest destiny that star marketing embraces. Historian Frederick Merk says this philosophy was born out of "a sense of mission to redeem the Old World by high example—generated by the potentialities of a new earth for building a new heaven." From my perspective, it's one thing to stare up at the night sky and be inspired by its beauty, its depth, and its eternal nature. It's another thing entirely to hawk the heavens in the name of love.

The online star registration site posts many happy reviews of its services, all of them one-liners, none of them with anything less than a five-star rating. I've read many of them and uncovered no complaints about the quality of a star, its inaccessibility, or the misspelling of a name. Customers seem to be pleased, holding this abstraction in their hearts while remaining tight-lipped about the specifics.

Like I said, I'm less inclined to see the business as a service to humankind, much less to the universe. What if, for example, I'm sold a dud, a star that went supernova ten-thousand years ago and all I can see when I glance at my purchase is its last breathtaking pulse of light spewed across the galaxy? Can I return my star for a refund? What if I want to upgrade, add the nearest star to my registry with plans to buy up an entire *gal-de-sac* and plot a new constellation with my own moniker? Will OSR work with me on keeping the undesirables out of my celestial neighborhood, or will the kinds of questions I'm asking define me as a consumer advocating trouble? More than likely the latter.

Take heart. At least I'm not disparaging the marketing behind Hollywood's Walk of Fame, a stretch of concrete and terrazzo with embedded brass stars dedicated to over 2,500 entertainers. This Chamber of Commerce's marketing scheme attracts millions of visitors annually, tourists who are excited to stare at their feet while paying tribute to their favorite personalities.

Fixed to nearly two miles of sidewalk, it is by far the more concrete approach to immortality.

FREIGHT FRIGHT

I ncreasingly, what we need we haven't got, and to get it to us requires a corporation. Post Office managers stamp their feet and manufacture more boxes. I don't know about you, but increased shipping costs have begun to make my health insurance premiums appear modest and affordable.

Probably the best delivery bargain left on the North American continent is still the post office's stamp for a single ounce letter, but so few people write letters anymore. Email, texting, cell phones, Zoom, and telepathy have all taken the place of a simple sincerely yours.

To take the sting out of continual rate increases, the post office has issued what they call the "forever stamp," which means if you purchase, say, $10,000 worth of first class stamps and squirrel them away in a dark drawer, you should be able to send your letter for the cost of a postage stamp back in the year you bought them—if trees, paper, and the post office still exist years later, of course. I can almost imagine thrifty old folks leaving their unused forever stamps to their grandchildren as part of their inheritance.

Another even more pessimistic interpretation of what the "forever" stands for is the eternal truth that all you can be certain of are death, taxes, and that shipping costs will continue to rise. UPS, FedEx, DHL—they're all in the same business, but the post office is the only shipper that seems to face eternal financial ruin. The private companies don't have to submit their rate increase proposals to anyone for approval. Their personnel might smile more, but cheerfulness has a price tag.

Recently, I purchased a license plate mount for the front bumper of my new used vehicle. I couldn't locate the proper mount locally, so I went to that digital warehouse called the internet to find one. The best I found was just over $30, a completely competitive price when compared with local auto suppliers' prices, but this one fit my bumper perfectly. I ordered it, thinking I'd gotten a bargain.

When shipping costs were calculated, the total came out to over $50. The plastic mount weighed a total of two pounds, which included its packaging! I don't even want to mention what the county clerk charged me for the license plate.

Of course, the cost of merchandise is steadily on the rise too, but more and more the monetary value of the product I'm shipping is actually less than the cost of the shipping itself. Carriers blame gas prices, which is a fair explanation, but that doesn't account for all those gougers out there whose profit margins are jacked up by shipping "and handling" charges that exceed the actual shipping costs—a detail often hidden from the purchaser even after the package arrives.

I mention all this because there's got to be a way to rein in the escalating cost of shipping, something that we as a consumer nation rely on more and more. Less and less of what we need is produced locally, or even within a reasonable distance from the place we call home, including the very food we put in our mouths. Santa Claus is not a workable solution, nor is the prospect of finding a *Star Trek* transporter beam online for the next generation.

Maybe we need what socially conscious politicians keep talking about with taxes, not just a flat rate but an equitable one. I mean, how can the businesses that send me such a continuous stream of junk-mail cluttering my mailbox ever afford to stay in business, unless the shipping rates I'm paying are out of whack with the bulk and commercial rates they're paying? What about a little transparency along with those tracking numbers? What kind of *mpp* (that's miles per package) is my little bundle getting by the time it arrives? If we don't fix it, the future of shipping might look like this:

"I'd like to ship this package, please.

"Certainly. How quickly do you want it to arrive?"

"Standard shipping will be fine."

"So, you don't care about the person who's receiving it?"

"Of course I care."

"Standard shipping is no way to show you care. May I recommend our triple upgrade."

"I just want it to arrive in good condition."

"Our triple upgrade guarantees that. The first upgrade makes sure it's on the correct truck, the second upgrade discourages abusive drivers from handling your delivery, and the third upgrade triples your shipping cost."

"Why would I want to triple my cost?"

"To show you care."

"I'll stick with standard shipping."

"That will be fifty dollars."

"Fifty dollars? How much with insurance?"

"A hundred and fifty."

"I'll drive it there myself for a hundred and fifty dollars."

"Excellent. If you'll back up to the loading dock before leaving, we have a few other packages traveling in your direction."

DUST THOU AIN'T

Yesterday, as I walked past our local funeral home, a young man—presumably an employee—tottered along the curb with one of those portable blower devices, raising a cloud of dust, sweeping down the street in a southernly direction. Unfortunately, the wind was coming from the south, so he reminded me of that character from the *Peanuts* comic strip named Pigpen. I shouldn't have laughed. It would have been kinder to catch up with him and, if possible, point him toward a different career.

You see, I can appreciate a windy day, especially in the fall, when autumn's leaves on the ground rattle and scrape against each other. There's always the faint possibility they'll get picked up by a dust devil, mulched, and redeposited on my garden where the soil always needs an amendment of compost. What rattles my teeth is not a cold wind out of the north, but that entirely artificial wind of a handheld gas blower accompanied by its godawful whine.

Remember those fall days of yore when raking the yard depleted only a few sweat glands and raised a couple blisters on your hands? Or just walking down the sidewalk kicking dry leaves like stacks of potato chips, tossing armfuls into the air and pretending the debris was confetti? It's possible rakes and brooms will become antiques, replaced by "blowers that are among the most powerful in the industry, designed to save you time and energy."

A generation or two from now children will see the traditional rake and broom leaning against a museum wall and ask, "What are those for?" They'll play with them as if they were toys, riding them like stick ponies, not understanding the years of wholesome chores such basic tools represented to their grandparents.

But I'm not inflexible. I'd join the blower revolution if it sucked. I mean, where do the blower people think the debris they set into motion gets deposited? It doesn't just disappear into the atmosphere like steam rising from a cup of coffee. Shopkeepers and neighbors who use these appliances to tidy up their property ought to look a bit further into the future. Everything four feet in front of them looks quite clean when they're finished, but the world slightly beyond their field of vision is appreciably dirtier.

The blower is only the tip of the dustbin, because our particulates fill the atmosphere wherever humans settle down. A haze of woodsmoke hovers over our winter towns. We start our engines and idly speculate about the rumor of global warming, as if it were a media war being waged by a foreign power. Carl Sandburg's poem might be amended in the desert Southwest to read, "The yellow fog that comes from the coal power plant on little cat feet, sits looking over the Four Corners on silent haunches and then moves on." You could learn to hate this kind of poetry if you lived downwind.

Sandburg also wrote, "When a nation goes down or a society perishes, one condition may always be found—they forgot where they came from." Perhaps we did come from dust, but with seven billion of us on the planet, a person has to wonder why, as a species, we are the ones blowing it. According to a ten-year U.S. Geological Survey study, the sand dunes of the Navajo Reservation— as many as nine thousand acres of sand—have begun an unusual migration, some of the dunes climbing up to 115 feet per year, all in a north-easterly direction, all because of long term drought, sparse vegetation, and unusually dry winds. The study doesn't mention if the winds are gas-powered.

I don't know who patented the design for a portable blower, but it reminds me of one of those splendidly useless kitchen gadgets that makes too much noise, takes up an inordinate amount of space, and only glorifies a pedestrian task.

It's also no surprise that the owner's manual for every blower sold recommends wearing a face mask and full-time protection against hearing loss. These instructions ought to be mandated for the rest of us living on the planet, rather than just requiring us to hold our breath, or scatter.

I realize the increasing use of leaf blowers does not mean the end of the world, but it does tend to raise the issue about "the dust unto which we shall return" a little prematurely.

WHEN PLASTIC BAGS ARE
BANNED

T he brown paper bag I carried out of the bookstore wasn't there for the sake of discretion. Truth be told, the bookstore refuses to handle plastic anymore. Ideally, the clerk told me, the store was on the verge of going entirely bagless, so I was lucky to be handed a brown paper sack. But it was raining—*fortunately* raining—and as I walked down the sidewalk trying to shield my new purchase, I secretly imagined a few genuine watermarks marring the surface of a page or two, indelible reminders that the spine of the West's summer drought had finally been broken.

When (and if) the electronic book revolution gets more flexible and affordable, this bookstore might also be going bookless. Despite our latest national fixation with banning disposable plastic bags, nobody knows exactly how the future will be packaged. From an ebook merchandiser's point of view, the traditional book is the archetype of excess packaging, the ideas on the page the only "product" an ecologically-minded consumer should have to purchase.

As a wordmonger, I tend to agree, but not entirely. Like a lot of people, I've been thinking that the earth would be a lot better off without plastic bags. At the time of their appearance in the consumer world, they were touted as cheaper, lighter, more durable, and a blessing when it came to saving trees. Now, as is the case with many innovations, they have become a blessing transformed into a curse. No matter where you live, plastic bags billow and blow like dried leaves across the landscape or clog up the rivers.

Allegedly, a hundred billion of them get tossed out annually, a one-use trip from the checkout line to the landfill. Major cities in the West, including Los Angeles, San Francisco, Portland and Seattle, legislated action to ban the plastic bag, some going so far as to charge shoppers ten cents and a nasty look if they begged for paper. Colorado tourist towns like Telluride and Durango have been waging letter-to-the-editor wars over local ordinances that would stifle a shopper's ability to get his or her hands on all but the credit card kind of plastic.

During these disposable bag debates, I wonder if anyone is talking about the sheer volume of packaging being hauled away inside those plastic and paper hammocks that cradle the products we buy, not to mention the shipping cartons and reams of plastic wrap that arrive by the semi-load at every shopping outlet before the merchandise gets arranged as stock on every American retail shelf.

Yes, there's plenty of waste to go around, but the burden of it manages to fall, once again, squarely in the shopper's cart.

I try to remember my reusable bags when I go out. Just like the fifteen pairs of reading glasses I tuck into every corner of my house, bags are stuffed all over my vehicle, in the trunk, under the seats, in the glove compartment, and I also compress them into the tiny pockets of my backpack and bicycle and scooter saddlebags. Yet somehow, inevitably, I sometimes end up standing bagless in the checkout line, forced to accept plastic bags or if I'm really lucky, increasingly rare paper bags, which come in handy as garbage-can liners. If plastic bag bans become the norm in the West, I'm guessing this new set of regulations will only prompt human beings to find sneakier ways around them.

After banning the bag, some cities have already reported increases in shoplifting, thanks to the influx of personal reusable sacks in their stores. Sadly, as long as saving money is the bottom line, the planet will never be our number one concern.

As a community, I know we should be more than semi-conscious about the problem, but then again, is anyone keeping track of how many customers reuse or recycle the plastic bags they collect in some form or another? I know we're offered secondhand bags with every secondhand purchase we make at garage sales and thrift stores. Surely, education—and not simply banning plastic bags—is key to solving the problem. Or am I a Pollyanna?

Although I may be compost before the average plastic bag breaks down, I can't help but foresee a future city or coastline where mounds of reusable tote bags—all discarded— have come to rest. Ah, someone will tell me, this is our newest unnatural wonder, the great dunes of our good intentions.

THE TEXTABLE THUMB

For a very long time in the civilization of humankind, elocution was the rage. It accounted for the human species's dominance over the less articulate creatures of the earth, but that trait has become passé, its social advantages laid bare now that natural selection has reengineered an older trait, one that pays less and less attention to its physical environment, choosing instead to rely on its codified digital presence and its opposable thumb.

I should disclose that I have very little training in science, even less in archaeology, and a pathetic grasp of the inner workings of technology. A version of Edward Snowden with secrets to share I am not, so my remarks on the practice of texting should be taken for what they're worth. If you have better things to do, please, by all means, do them, even if one of them is checking to see if someone has sent you a text.

Let me also say I have never sent a text message, which further establishes me as a technological Neanderthal, but in my defense, let it be known that I own an iPad, so the idea of texting is not completely foreign to me. Let's just say, I have equipment that has allowed me, for example, to type using my thumbs (both at the same time!) and I found the experience less than satisfying, a bit like eating a bowl of shredded wheat with a set of butter knives.

The internet claims the fastest speed for texting—twenty-six words in 43.24 seconds—was set by a twenty-three-year-old woman from Singapore. Then, a woman from Britain beat her record before a man from Singapore typing on a touch screen beat both, but I suspect anonymous and unaware individuals are breaking that record every day. After all, contests like the U.S. National Texting Championship only declare winners from among those who enter the competition. In the backwaters, perhaps along a tranquil section of irrigation ditch here in the West, a virtual Shakespeare may surface one day, one who texts with both speed and style.

On the average, a teenager sends over 3,200 messages a month, an equivalent to roughly 103 phone calls a day. I admit that comparing text messages to phone calls may seem unfair, but only because texters find actual, auditory conversation on a phone uncomfortable. The spontaneity of what to say or what might be said reportedly makes hardline texters feel unnerved. The text message provides a more controllable experience, one where a reply may be thought about or edited or deleted.

Sadly, the extinction of this textable-thumb species is a certainty, and I'm not talking about those individuals who were filmed falling into fountains or stepping off subway platforms onto electrified tracks while operating their personal devices. Nor am I talking about the ones who simply text while driving. Clearly, behaviors like these will lead to sudden ends for these misfits, along with many innocents who are in the wrong place at the wrong time, but not necessarily for the species as a whole.

Another factor I'm *not* talking about is the carpal tunnel crippler once nicknamed Blackberry Thumb. It's more descriptively referred to as a common repetitive strain injury, and because the thumb has so much less dexterity than the fingers, texters may be more prone to suffer with the aches and throbbing pains of the wrist. It may slow the species down, but it definitely won't lead to its extinction.

It also may be that the textable thumb will survive long enough to provide an identifiable characteristic, like the slight adaptations in beak shapes that Darwin noticed among his finches while visiting the Galapagos Islands. Texters may discover that the nails on their thumbs will cease to grow, or, from setting their phones on vibrate, they may develop a hypersensitive awareness to the slightest earth tremors, which may lead to the first human seismograph.

In the end, however, everything the texter has accomplished by adapting to a more oblique way of life will be rendered moot, because technology evolves faster than any species can anticipate. What's next? A chip implanted in the eyelid? A router routed where we don't even want to speculate? A genome that lights up a cellular universe, brighter than Sirius?

Perhaps in the undisclosed future, an unborn child might ask his father, "How did humans communicate with each other before telepathy?"

His father might reply, "Son, they used to text with their thumbs."

"What's a thumb?"

SOLSTICE

At the annual winter solstice bonfire we stood around a mound of dry limbs, wrapped in layers of material warmth, anxious for that moment when the fire finally catches and the crisp branches burst into bright orange flames, all of us waiting to be overwhelmed by a rush of fire and light. The man beside me, blowing into his ungloved hands as if he held a bird's nest, leaned toward me to ask a flinty question.

"At what exact time does the solstice finally begin?" December 21st is officially the shortest day of the year, but at what point in time the curtain between autumn and winter gets drawn is anyone's guess? At least I had no idea.

Leaving my hands jammed deep into my pockets, I leaned back and shouted very loudly at the star-speckled sky.

"Hey Siri, what time does the solstice begin?" Suddenly I became the center of attention. Eyes shifted from the woody pyre. I shrugged. The man beside me stepped away, just a bit. Then he clapped his hands and laughed.

"I get it, a cosmic technology joke!"

Just then, the fire rushed up its rickety ladder of limbs and stood nearly fifty-feet tall, a behemoth clothed in light. I thought, well, maybe now is as good a time as any.

I'm actually pleased that Siri wasn't listening via any plug-in to the stars, and that Alexa was napping, perhaps in the back of an Amazon delivery truck, or that Google Assistant had more important inquiries, like discovering its own moniker, and that Microsoft's Cortana hadn't yet fully answered to its role as the universe's personal assistant. You see, if I wanted a voice-activated secretary, I would probably have adopted a dog. Possibly a pit bull.

So hackers be warned, those of you who have broken new ground into the surveillance world by illegally accessing home cameras. Ring devices, for example, have been named in a class-action lawsuit that cites a lack of due diligence by Ring, and especially Amazon, in providing "robust" security protections for their customers. I don't know which side will prevail in the lawsuit, but sadly—despite the absurdity of revealing one's presence by talking to his victims—the hackers are not being sued or held accountable for their actions.

Smart phones, iPads and Android tablets, smart televisions, and even your not-so-smart ding-dong doorbell contain serious flaws, enough to allow criminals into your personal world without much technical effort, partly because users often fail to update security protocols, and especially because we are often too lazy or uninformed about changing the default passwords that came with our devices. Manufacturers continue to defend themselves by explaining in no uncertain terms: default is yours.

A bonfire, however, is the antithesis of technology. It's a primitive combustible pile of organic stuff that will burn anyone and anything that gets too close. A spectacle so hot any terms of service or privacy policy would not allow the user to get close enough to agree to the risks.

Sleepy, disoriented neighbors glancing out their windows, for instance, might mistake the glow for sunrise. Police and fire personnel might grow anxious if the party's host fails to call ahead, advising them of their plans.

Yet if we take all the obvious precautions, rake debris from around the bonfire site so sparks won't ignite a brushfire, and arrange a garden hose within easy reach, we are still in danger. In order to be prepared for an emergency, my friend showed me how to locate the faucet valve and turn the hose on. If he could say he retrofitted the old technology and invented a smart faucet, his mistake was that he told me.

Maybe the instinct to surround ourselves with cameras and automated, instantaneous answers to our every whim has been instinctively lodged within us since the beginning of human time. You know, that endless "search for meaning" in the chaotic universe. Our cave forefathers and foremothers stared into the fire like we gaze into our backlit phone screens and hope that someone is actually listening.

Of course, theological and technological presences are hardly the same thing. The parable of Steve Jobs, for instance, lacks a moral depth when compared to the Book of Job. Profits and prophets are so easily confused, although biblically Job does end up with all his money returned, plus additional wealth for obeying the directive. His economic boon allows us to disregard his misery.

As technologies advance at an unprecedented pace, we may have reason to feel disoriented, or "disconnected" by our social media. As the old 1990s Virginia Slims cigarette commercial phrased it, we may have "come a long way, baby" but surely we are still playing with fire.

SAFETY FIRST

I'd just settled into the doctor's consulting room after a nurse checked and recorded my vitals. The door closed softly after her promise that it wouldn't be long. I glanced around at the colorful charts of body parts, their maladies graphically depicted alongside their normal, healthy appearances. The room was a kiosk of frightening information, but I couldn't concentrate. I needed a bathroom.

Knowing the doctor was on her way, I decided to wait. In any person's daily life, choosing when to use a bathroom is usually uncomplicated. The urge to go is often followed closely by the going. But medical exams upstage habit. It's essential, for instance, that a patient arrive on time, but the morning never goes smoothly. You oversleep. The coffee machine has a tantrum. Your driveway turns into a Möbius strip because you forget an important medical form on the kitchen table and are forced to execute a sudden U-turn in front of a startled school-bus driver. Then, the parking lot at the hospital is packed with vehicles. You wonder if a large-scale disaster is unfolding and nobody bothered to mention it. So, you park a distance away and hike to the door, wheezing like a two-pack-a-day smoker by the time you climb the stairs and stand sweating before the receptionist to announce you're here for your ten o'clock appointment.

Being left alone in the consulting room meant I was nearly finished with this waiting. I'll postpone the bathroom urge for a few more minutes, I told myself. It's a routine follow-up visit after all, involving a peek at the afflicted area, a few questions, and a promise to meet again in three weeks to a month. Then, someone paused in the hall outside the exam room. I expected the door to open but a high-pitched alarm started screeching, piercing the air as a bright white light flashed on the wall above me.

Oh shit, the makings of an evacuation. I decided to sit quietly and hope it went away. It didn't. A nurse entered and said I'd have to join the stream of people leaving the building. "Continue along the corridor and go out to the parking lot," she instructed.

"What's going on?" I asked, but she suddenly turned to usher other people toward their salvation.

Before I retired, I'd been a part of formalized evacuations for twenty-seven years as a public school teacher. Usually, they were pre-scheduled. I was supposed to act as part of a team, clearing the building as quickly as possible. For many years, only fire drills. Eventually bomb drills were added to the fire drill practice, then lockdowns so drug dogs could check the students' lockers, then we were taught to hide the students in a darkened classroom and keep them quiet after locking the door to practice responding to the hypothetical threat of an armed shooter in the building. We memorized codes that would be announced over the PA system, color schemes to measure the severity of the hypothetical situation. The more we practiced, the more my students refused to take any emergency seriously. They'd giggle with each other in the dark, pretend to scream out of terror, then giggle some more.

Our commitment to fighting the crazies demands us to be prepared, and well we should be, but instead of coaching our children in the strategies of becoming lifelong careful observers of their surroundings, we drill them in rote exercises to elicit a mass, mindless reaction. Go where you are told. Don't ask questions. Depend on somebody else knowing what to do. I'm amazed we aren't still insisting they hide under their desks and cover their heads.

All these thoughts ran through my brain as I headed toward the exit, but then I noticed a set of bathroom doors in an alcove near the elevator. I slowed my pace, drifted toward the wall, and watched for a gap in the foot traffic. When the opportunity arrived, I slipped into a bathroom, closed, and locked the door.

Once again, I examined the minuscule proportions of my new surroundings. Stuck to a strip of Velcro on the wall above the door I spotted a piece of plastic shaped like a motel Do Not Disturb notice. It had one printed word: Evacuated.

Considering my own urgency, I realized it was a perfect word to have fixed to the wall in a public bathroom.

As I left, I ripped the sign from its Velcro mount and hung it on the doorknob, doing my part to steer the world away from another dangerous place.

DOMESTIC ARCHAEOLOGY

J ust like the noted Egyptologist, Howard Carter—the one who discovered King Tut's mummified remains surrounded by a breathtaking array of splendid treasures—except in my case, no treasures. All I'd come nose-to-nose within the dim tomb-like confines turned out to be the desiccated carcass of a cat that had never belonged to me. I bagged the corpse and dragged it out of the crawl-space. Then, sucking a few more gulps of fresh air, I went back in to fix a leaking water pipe.

They say there are no atheists in foxholes, a senti-ment that must hold true for crawlspaces. As a boy raised in the Midwest, I experienced full basements. My subterranean subconscious tells me they still stand for stalwart tornado shelters, laundry rooms, workshops, and root cellars. But a crawlspace? Not until moving to the Southwest.

My catacomb-like expanse stretched out the length of our doublewide trailer, yet barely two feet high. Previous owners had skirted it with stacked field stones, then plastered the stones together with cement. The outside sunlight filtered through myriad holes and cracks where the cement had fallen away. Spiderwebs hung like beaded curtains. I absolutely did not want to be in that space and had avoided it for years. In fact, when we first purchased the place, it required only a cursory peek behind the access flap to assure me that nothing could possibly go wrong under there!

Of course, sewer lines seep, pipes freeze, critters creep, and snakes slither. It is deterioration enhanced by human nature's practice to build as cheaply as possible. Clean crawlspaces actually exist, with vapor barriers and tight foundations footings, leveling and lighting, but not where I've lived. One home I inspected came with the equivalent of a bear den under the floor, another with a set of trenches straight out of the history books from World War I. The town of Cortez, where I live, enjoys an average of 240 sunny days annually, but there are dark places people don't talk about.

The only way to reach my water pipes required unrolling a long black avenue of sheet plastic which I pulled myself along, using its slickness against my back while grabbing the undercarriage of the mobile home's metal frame. Dust clouded my vision with each foot of progress. My partner in excavation stood somewhere above me tapping a broomstick against the kitchen floor, emitting a kind of wooden sonar designed to help me locate the offending leak. I wore a headlamp like a miner, its beam punctuating my fright each time it lighted on some creepy shadow off in the distance.

The dirt floor was littered with rusted cans, beer bottles, mason jars, useless lengths of pipe, a Barbie doll, crumpled and yellowed newspaper, and shards of tin, all amid the rubble of wood and concrete blocks that once propped up the trailer's frame. I began to suspect that a hidden trapdoor existed somewhere in the floor above me where former residents simply dropped their trash. How else could this mess have arrived? I wasn't sure.

With a shudder of despair, I noticed that no cables had been secured to keep the trailer from flying away in Wizard-of-Oz-ish fashion, so I knew I'd be underneath again, tethering my worries. Then, the critter agenda manifested itself, a gap in the stones where an unidentified flurry of furry critters had left evidence of their visitations. My headlamp swept the area like a searchlight, expecting to find a set of glowing eyes staring back at me. All I found reflected was a dusty soda bottle tipped on its side, only the crescent of its bottom still visible above the soft dirt like a new moon on its way to ground.

Eventually, I located and fixed the pipe, which proved to be much easier than I'd expected. The task required all my concentration, so all the ghosts receded from my imagination as I shuttled back and forth along my plastic slide, retrieving the tools I needed.

But I should also mention the curse that manifested itself as a result of opening the crawlspace. Every time I even think about going back down there, trickles of sweat work their way down my temples. When I think about something else, they go away. Imagine that.

DONE WITH THIS PLANET?

A few weeks after the Mars InSight touched down on the red planet's surface, I clicked a computer audio link that captured two minutes and twenty-seven seconds of a Martian wind. The idea of opening an electronic window and listening as a breeze at least 33.9 million miles away nuzzled NASA's robotic sensors initially appealed to me, but in less than a minute I started getting bored. The recording was not so different from what I hear any day when the wind is blowing outside my earthly window.

Will boredom be our species's salvation? When Charles Darwin wrote, "Building a better mousetrap merely results in smarter mice," he might have been thinking about our destiny. He also observed, "The world will not be inherited by the strongest, it will be inherited by those most able to change."

And we are changing, but for good or bad, I'm not sure. A Microsoft Corporation study found that since the turn of the millennium our average attention span has reduced from twelve seconds to eight seconds. I can corroborate this finding. My paragraphs keep getting shorter.

But the science of measuring attention spans has also been questioned, with good reason. The headline "You Now Have A Shorter Attention Span Than A Goldfish" is written for shock value. The facts lack some credibility, because the length of time during which one is able to concentrate or remain interested has always depended on the subject of focus, and goldfish lack the ability to provide scientists with a meaningful appendage to count web-browser or re-mote-control clicks with anything other than their tail fins.

Is the earth changing? Whether you believe polar ice is melting, or that earth's ozone layer is receding faster than my hairline is not the point. It's more important to note that a growing number of human beings are getting bored with even hearing about climate news.

Once upon a time, my father's admonishment when I complained of boredom was, "There are no uninterest-ing things, only uninterested people." A rather unchar-acteristically thoughtful remark from my father. When I found out he stole that bit of wisdom from G. K.

Chesterton, I finally understood why he usually told me to go read a book.

But really, I did make an effort to listen to the entire wind recording. I even closed my eyes and tried tele-porting to the planet, as if Martian ghosts gentled by immeasurable time might start whispering to me. Mind you, I'm not saying I discovered life on Mars. NASA isn't saying so either. But that sound bite established some sort of bridge between our planets, reducing the imaginative distance that divides our worlds.

Ray Bradbury's *The Martian Chronicles* evokes the tragedy of conquest, earthlings fleeing one doomed planet for the sake of infesting another. Throughout the novel, remnants of Martian civilization speak to the colonists in haunting voices, reminding them in both touching and horrific ways of what's been lost. Brad-bury's book is fiction, of course, but told in such a way as to jog our memories, which also appear to be getting shorter when it comes to avoiding the colossal mistakes we have historically made.

I can't imagine anything more odious than volun-teering to commute to a different planet for the sake of colonizing it. Besides, it would take at least half a year to reach Mars—in some cases even longer—and would require a mountain of in-flight peanuts. Some people might say it makes more sense to take the same interest in our own planet's welfare, to commit to the notion that the earth is a finite resource, that human beings themselves are increasingly becoming a disposable commodity.

If we are merely bored with our globe, revitalizing and reinvesting in our human curiosity is a worthy goal. Certainly, NASA research has benefitted humanity, providing new products and approaches for earthlings that don't require us to occupy a space station or another planet to reap their benefits. But dismissing what science tells us about what's happening to the earth is folly. All our nifty little gadgets, especially that short-lived mind-numbing fidget spinner fad, only occupy our fingers. Have we forgotten how to actually see with our eyes?

Admittedly, we've been fascinated by space exploration for a long time, from Jules Verne's vision of shooting a missile at the moon to the great space race between Russia and America that spawned Sputnik. Rockets ignited and tempers flared. Astronauts became heroes for putting their lives on the line and venturing into the unknown. But we need another kind of hero, one who is blessed with the kind of insight that's not necessarily needed to drive a Mars rover, one that can translate what Mars has to say about us as caretakers of this planet.

When I step out to the porch in the evening and stare at the sparkling heavens, nothing thrills me more than suddenly noticing that my feet are both firmly planted on this bedrock, this hearth, this home.

THE NEXT BRIGHT IDEA

The light fixture in my bathroom blew a bulb. To fully illuminate the mirror, three bulbs were required. Instead of simply replacing the single burned-out bulb and waiting like an audience for the chorus line's next kick, I splurged and bought twelve LED replacements.

When I opened the box, I was disappointed. The bulbs looked like an ordinary cardboard carton of Large Grade A eggs, and according to the colorful packaging, LEDs are the "best" choice for both saving money on utilities and for saving the environment. I changed out the entire row and I didn't hear a squawk.

This episode occurred in 2018. At that time, I paid a shocking price for the replacements until I factored in their advertised average lifespan of nine to twenty-two years. I'd be well into my seventh decade before I'd need to replace another bathroom bulb. By then, scientists might have invented a roll of toilet paper that lasts twenty years.

Too soon, however, the hype fizzled. Three months into one bulb's first birthday, a flicker developed that lasted for about five seconds every time I flipped the switch. This continued for weeks (although it felt like months) until the bulb simply gave up. I replaced what must have been a defective product with one of the hallowed nine standbys until, a month later (although it felt like a year), a different bathroom bulb quite suddenly went dark. I was down to eight. And because lightbulbs in a chorus line all look the same, and because LED technology burns relatively cool compared to incandescent bulbs, I decided to inscribe a tiny indelible "2018" near the base of the last bulb standing. Like a lightbulb, I'd be screwed if I could remember which one was the sole survivor a decade later.

Fast forward to 2020. I bought my second LED twelve-pack. In two years the price had come down a little, but how time burns. The advertised life expectancy must be calculated in dog years, each actual year an equivalent of seven LED years.

I should also mention that my brain has a tendency to run a bit medieval, like it did in 2007 when the government phased out incandescent light bulbs. I wondered if we might be heading toward another dark age, but an international ban on this older technology did not dim the world's lights. Quite the opposite. Consumers simply chose an alternative technology for their lighting needs.

The "ban" on incandescent bulbs never made selling them illegal. They still show up in thrift stores, and the dark alleys of black-market smuggling haven't emerged because selling contraband light-bulbs for profit is obviously not a bright idea. The change was ushered in by a simple law that required manufacturers to deliver a product that met better energy use standards, and, as any adult living during the transitional period knows, solutions often illuminate new problems.

Halogen bulbs, for example, use twenty-eight percent less energy but they burn hotter than comparable incandescents, which not only increases fire risk but also reduces the bulb's longevity to a year or two. CFL (fluorescent) bulbs provide a seventy-five percent energy use savings and a much longer life, but the inferior quality of light they produce persuaded me to avoid them. I've also noticed that hotels and motels use these bulbs almost exclusively, which might explain why customers aren't tempted to steal them. Still, the deal-killer for me is a dangerous neurotoxin called mercury, turning their use and disposal into a potential health issue.

The flaws in these alternative technologies explain why LEDs have rapidly dominated the marketplace. Besides being dimmable, directional, suitable for many design applications, shatter-resistant and more affordable, an eighty-five percent energy use reduction is what the world needs. As for the popular belief that each bulb lasts a long time, the jury is still out. To compensate for my disappointment, I've adopted a new goal: to outlive my lightbulbs.

Other toxic technologies like coal, oil, auto emissions, pesticides, aerosols, certain plastics used in manufacturing food containers and bottles, chemicals in cosmetics, antiperspirants, dry-cleaning, and nuclear waste need to be legislated out of existence, a legacy that makes living a long life also worthwhile. Meanwhile, I have a few bulbs left in my second box of LED replacements, and I'll surely buy another box before the end of the year.

As you can tell, I am interested in all forms of illumination. The very word reminds me that medieval scribes spent much of their lives elaborately decorating manuscripts with ink and paint, then gilding the panels with silver and gold. Not many of these masterpieces survived, and those that did are rare museum artifacts, salvaged from history, perhaps by serfs who pilfered them from wealthy estate bookshelves but could not get them to burn as efficiently as wood.

7: Borrowing From the Past Again

A CAUTIONARY TALE

A warning two miles before I saw the flaggers should have alerted me: standard road construction, orange cones, black tar, tens-of-thousands of pixels dancing on the surface of a digital road sign, all of them screaming caution. But I did not expect the early sun to rise so suddenly above the tree line as the pavement curved east, and once I entered the curve the sunlight shattered my visibility.

Luckily, I had seen the first notice advising me to slow down, but traffic in front of me had already come to a dead stop. The screech of my tires reverberated off the surrounding tree trunks. The flagger jumped back, as if he were playing a game of frogger, and I could feel a half dozen eyes glaring at me in their respective side mirrors.

Sorry, I said aloud, although I was by myself. Then, I shut off the engine, slouched, and pretended to be fiddling with my seatbelt. As an afterthought, I switched my flashers on, then as an after-afterthought I switched them back off when it occurred to me that they'd only draw more attention my way.

It turned out to be a long delay, vehicles stacking up behind me so far that I couldn't see the end of the line. By the time the traffic started forward, even the flagger had forgotten which car sponsored his heart's early morning jump-start. I waved as I drove past, and he waved back with his entire hand, not with his middle finger.

Finally, beyond the reach of roadwork, careening along at sixty-five miles an hour, I got to thinking about my little lapse in judgment, which only made me feel foolish, that a man like me who'd recently turned sixty-five couldn't be trusted to drive at that speed.

By now I could see far enough down the imaginary road to the spot where the authorities were forced to wrestle the driver's license from my clenched fingers, ordering me to be reasonable, to behave like a mature member of the Older Drivers Division. My bumper by then would have been painted hunter's orange, a legal requirement for ODD drivers like me wishing to remain behind the wheel beyond retirement age.

No doubt special hours for older drivers would apply—prohibiting the operation of a motor vehicle after dark or during inclement weather or driving while medicated. Public service announcements along the highways would urge drivers to call 665 if they needed to report a geezer.

I know, it's all more than a few years away, but I've always expected delays. According to the Census Bureau, the number of statistically mature people between 2004 and 2050 is expected to increase 147 percent, from 36.3 to 86.7 million Americans traveling down life's highway at sixty-five or more. These folks—in a few years, *my* folks—will comprise twenty-one percent of the country's population, but what startles me most is realizing that I could still be alive in the year 2050.

Imagine that! My gene pool could theoretically make it possible, because my father possessed a valid driver's license up to the day he expired—when he was ninety-four. As father and son, however, we were not of similar minds. I inherited his car, a Pontiac Grand Am, with a spoiler on the trunk lid, dual exhausts, bucket seats, a six-cylinder engine, custom wheels, and a CD player he never used because he only trusted cassettes. He could have ordered a car to come with a cassette player when he made the purchase, but he didn't like to wait. He drove it home the same day, and nothing except a broken hip ever slowed him down.

Since 1963, the government's Administration on Aging officially designates the month of May as Older Americans Month. The theme for my sixty-fifth year, in case you missed it, was Unleash the Power of Age. I wish they would have asked me before choosing that theme. I'm not comfortable with the word Unleash. It makes me think of domestic pets, and I'm plagued by the image of tiny dogs jumping up and down on the furniture, the epitome of impatience.

The next time I'm sitting in a line of traffic, waiting for the flagger to flip the sign from Stop to Slow, glancing in my rearview mirror as the line of cars lengthens, I'll be thinking of the untapped power behind me. Once we finally begin moving forward, I might even pretend that I'm participating in a little parade, our batteries recharging as our brakes are released, as we gently accelerate toward our next obstacle with aging.

MY LUCKY STARS

I pulled into the motel parking lot, shut off my engine, and looked around without stepping out of the truck. From a distance, I thought the motel might qualify for a three-star rating, but after a closer look I decided no, it likely deserved no more than two stars, and that without seeing what the inside of a room looked like.

Many travelers would have accelerated down the road. I got out of the truck and walked toward the office. The "Vacancy" sign sputtered like the burner on an old gas stove and I was warmed by the thought that the place at least had its electricity on. The lobby stood unlocked but empty. I approached the check-in desk, tapped the bell. A slightly disheveled woman emerged from behind a beaded curtain.

"Do you have a room for the night?" I asked. A rhetorical question. Of course, she had a room. The motel included fifty or more rooms, I guessed, with only five vehicles in the parking lot. In exchange for handing her my credit card, I would be rewarded with a key to open a door leading to a few basic amenities.

My trip from my hometown of Cortez formed an awkward circle, taking me east over Wolf Creek Pass, with overnight stops in Alamosa and Trinidad, then south across the New Mexico border with a stay in Taos before heading back home. Scenery so exquisite it wouldn't all fit into my camera, but the memory of my motel accommodations left me thinking I should tell someone about this road experiment. Every time I brought up the subject of my recent lodgings at sleazy motels, friends feigned a mental rash and ran out the room.

The better lodgings these days line themselves up like dominos on the outskirts of towns large and small. But I'd decided before I left home that I wanted to stay in the old town centers whenever I could, where the nightlife was once lively but perhaps wasn't so much anymore. In megalopolis America, historic city centers often receive revitalization cash, but in small-town Colorado and New Mexico, main streets have been left to harbor a slightly seedy appearance.

I didn't know, for instance, that bedbugs inhabit some of these dives, not until I returned home and discovered a bedbug registry internet site while attempting to research a few historic details concerning one of my motel stops. The site invites users to search for motels by name or location.

Of my three overnight beds, two offered me a comforting assurance that no bedbug encounters had been recorded, which meant I'd lodged at one motel that did. For the next half hour I looked at pictures of bedbugs, forgetting about my original search for historic landmark photographs. If you haven't seen a bedbug magnified on a computer screen, you owe yourself an encounter.

Luckily, no bedbugs surfaced at my home, in my luggage, or on my person, so I don't have anything to report, but I feel obligated to mention a few other irregularities from my motel road trip.

One eye-opener involved a swimming pool—its gate securely locked, I should add—filled to the brim with stagnant water so green and thick with algae it surprised me that frogs weren't croaking from king-and queen-sized lily pads. This pool hadn't been used in years, a piece of history soured by some great loss, economic or otherwise, I guessed.

Another curiosity—and it ticked me off a bit—involved clocks, or rather, the complete lack of them.

Not one of my three motel rooms offered even a cheap plastic portal into time. Without a doubt, the motels themselves were time capsules, and while showering I couldn't stop singing Chicago's lyrics, "Does anybody really know what time it is? Does anybody really care?" Here? Obviously not. Perhaps the type of guests who stay at places like these steal anything not nailed down. Then I asked myself, "So why are you staying here?" I glanced around the room, taking a quick inventory, but nothing appeared all that tempting.

My next road trip might involve just a tent or an exposed patch of night sky above a swaying hammock. Spiders and ants. A gob of tree sap or bird shit in my hair, who knows. I'm still welcome at the motels where I stayed, because I didn't complain or post any two-star reviews. After all, even the universe is deteriorating, one star at a time.

OVEREATERS OBLIVIOUS

Now that the holidays are over—the *big* eating holidays, like Thanksgiving, Christmas, and the solid weeks of finishing off leftovers—we thought we'd be able to have a meal again as normal people were supposed to, at a restaurant, dining instead of cooking. We decided on a little buffet that friends recommended.

And it was true, the mashed potatoes, peas, fried chicken, and meat loaf looked a little better than ordinary, so we didn't hesitate to fork over our money to the friendly buffet cashier.

"It looks like you're ready to feed an army," I remarked.

"Nobody goes away hungry," the cashier replied.

We paid for the all-you-can-eat dinner special, picked up a clean plate, and started heaping it with various entrees.

"These sure are unusual serving spoons," Pam remarked.

"Yeah, they're pretty unusual," I replied, but I was concentrating on the lasagna. Having maximized the surface of the plate by arranging layers for each of the seven food groups, we sat down at our table to eat. We'd been raised in the Midwest and so the lesson of eating properly and consuming all that was on our plate constituted a way of life. Little conversation transpired, except for brief comments like, "Try this," or "Yum," or a simple jab with a knife— communication designed to enhance the eating process and not lead toward the discussion of serious ideas.

We excavated our way through the seven layers until, as our parents had instructed many times over, we had cleaned our plates.

"I think I'll go back for a little more of that pudding," I said.

"The roast beef looked tender," Pam replied.

We returned to the buffet line, picked up new plates, and as is common in buffet lines, intended to take less food on this second trip. But this was no ordinary buffet line. The serving spoons were indeed unusual. As spoons, the handles were specially shaped to comfortably fit the hand, and the spoons themselves were deep and allowed for a heaping portion to be scooped every time. In fact, these spoons would not allow themselves to be used in a dainty, petite manner. If a customer wanted only one cherry tomato to garnish the plate, the spoons refused to discriminate: they simply lunged into the food and came up with an impressive quantity of vegetables.

We had never handled spoons like these and so we came away from the line holding plates heaped with as much food as they held on our first trip through the line. Naturally, as people raised in Minnesota are taught, we felt obliged to eat everything on our plates.

"A little dessert would be nice," Pam said.

"I might try one more spoon of that pudding," I replied.

We returned to the buffet line, grabbed new plates, and as we walked past the main entries, the spoons went wild, jumping from the trays and heaping our plates with generous portions of the same food we'd already eaten twice.

"They're sure not skimpy here," I said.

"It's a pretty good value," Pam replied.

Of course, we ate everything on our plates and pushed them toward the center of the table, convinced we'd eaten all we could eat and that we'd certainly gotten our money's worth. But this time, the spoons levitated in the air and carried heaping servings of steaming food directly to our table. Nothing could be done except to eat what was before us, and so we reluctantly picked up our forks and began to clear our plates once again.

This time, however, the spoons refused to let our plates be emptied, and the food kept coming, spoon after spoon, and no matter how fast or slow we chewed, the spoons kept pace.

"I'm getting a little full," Pam remarked."

"Yeah, me too," I replied, or rather, mumbled with a mouthful.

But we kept eating, because people were starving all over the world, and the spoons knew only their job of serving the hungry.

LEGENDS OF MY FALL

A black-and-white eight-millimeter movie clip loops in my head: my ninety-four-year-old father is standing on a ladder, pruning the maple in his front yard. The exact time is unclear, because I wasn't there, so I've relied on reports from my siblings, but his last fall gets replayed in my head every autumn as the mountain aspens flicker like pilot lights.

He supported the ladder on the same limb he decided to prune. They both went down, without witnesses. He must have groaned, lost his wind, then sucked a healthy portion of air as he regained the world. Hard to tell, because the film has no sound, and the camera spends too much time zooming in on the top rung of the ladder, magnifying his mistake.

Foreshadowing can become a heavy-handed technique, a conjurer's trick that grants mere mortals a glimpse of the god-like power of omniscience. It's also a kind of artificial intelligence, because it doesn't exist in our day-to-day lives. If it did, we'd all be frantic to edit the scenes of our most awkward moments.

Or maybe genetics is nature's way of hinting about the future. Either way, some of my most breathtaking regrets have been sponsored by missteps and faulty observations.

I should pay closer attention to details. Bicycle crashes, tumbles down stairs, stumbling over my discarded shoes—the short list of personal collisions. My third-grade teacher, Sister Winifred, reserved a wide butter knife in the school's freezer so she could minister to my lumps. Apparently prayer proved inadequate when it came to reducing the swelling.

People who are unfamiliar with walking beside me occasionally reach out to steady me as one of my ankles folds like a pocket knife. I know—but they don't—that these unexpected wobbles are just part of my gait, or what I prefer to call "hockey moves."

In fairness to my father, I should disclose my own blunder. My second-story cedar shingles needed to be stained. The sun had bleached them to the color of bone. I deployed my massive extension ladder, the one I can barely carry out of the barn. I locked the rungs in place, leaned the entire contraption against the side of house, grabbed my brush, a bucket of stain, and started the climb toward heaven.

Either the lawn was damp or the ground too soft, but when I reached the top of the ladder it shifted, started to lean, then slid sideways. That's how I ended up plummeting, the ladder barely missing me during its descent, shattering a first story window on its way down.

When I hit the grass, all the fall colors flashed in my brain, but what I vividly remember seeing as I managed to roll over onto my back was a pattern like a Rorschach inkblot test that a gallon of redwood stain made as it splashed against the white vinyl siding. Psychologists might have had a field day with that image, interpreting the rationale for my unconscious attraction to death. I blame the ladder. Not that particular ladder, and not the genetic strand of aluminum twisting all the way back to the one my father unfolded to prune his tree. Any ladder possesses the mojo to shake a climber loose like a dry leaf from an autumn tree.

Nearly a hundred thousand people are taken to emergency rooms every year for injuries their ladders inflict. Fractures are the most common type of trouble.

My father broke his hip, but because he always resisted doctor offices, nobody knew. He treated himself with aspirin for six weeks until my siblings insisted he seek a medical opinion. X-rays revealed the fracture, and an operation repaired it. During his recovery, he was temporarily moved out of his home to an assisted living facility. He seemed to be doing fine.

When my brother visited, together they watched a football game in the lounge. Because of a head cold, my brother returned home before the end of the game. My father went back to his room. Care-givers found him on the floor, gone, only five days before the winter solstice. They assumed his heart had given out, that perhaps the stress of surgery followed by his body's attempted recovery had taken its toll on his old ticker. Nobody could say for sure.

I still blame the ladder.

NEVER MIND

"How's your earring?" an acquaintance at the coffee shop counter asks me. For a minute I'm confused. Of course, I recognize who he is, but I've never had either ear pierced. I'm about to say so, telling him that he's mistaken about my lobes and the ornaments he thinks might hang there when what he's really asking suddenly dawns on me. He wants to know how my hearing is doing— it's been three months since my ear surgery.

The answer to his question must be obvious without uttering a word. My face—flushed with the embarrassment of having wandered off a straight and well-lit mental path—is a dead giveaway. I want to explain, "No, it's not a symptom of early onset Alzheimer's." I want to shuffle my feet and do that little *ta-da!* dance step to suggest my stupid look has all been a vaudeville act. But instead, I glance at the floor, not sure what to say. He touches my shoulder, grabs his coffee-to-go, then goes.

The learning curve for coming to grips with this gradual dimming of my auditory self has taken a long time. Blame the hearing loss on too many decibels of Def Leppard, working in the company of rackety machinery, or shooting my pneumatic staple gun in the wrong direction.

Whatever the cause, the origin of the problem has lost all sense of importance. What I want to figure out now is how to behave so I don't end up as a reincarnation of my father-in-law who insisted until the day he left this earth that his hearing problem was simply everyone else's inability to speak up. I vividly remember when I first noticed his disconnect with a sound reality.

Newlyweds nearly forty years ago, Pam and I traveled to Chicago for a family visit. He'd mixed gin fizzes and we'd all moved outside to occupy lawn chairs. Sitting directly across from us, he delivered a lecture about "educated dummies" being left in charge of America's schools. I had just taken my first teaching job. Maybe he was trying to get on my good side by choosing a topic that held my interest.

Thankfully, an O'Hare airport flight path arced directly over his Arlington Heights residence. One minute I could hear him, the next minute any semblance of what he might be saying had been obliterated by the roar of a jet. The din prompted by the plane's passing amazed me, but what surprised me even more during its full minute of ascent was that my father-in-law's lips never stopped moving. He just continued explaining what was wrong with education, as if the bell jar we call the heavens had not been temporarily shattered.

Presbycusis is the word for a gradual hearing loss that occurs as people get older, one in three from the ages of sixty-five to seventy-four, nearly half of those over the age of seventy-five. Because this kind of loss is gradual, many age-related hearing problems sneak up on us, prompting people like my father-in-law to be stuck in a state of denial.

The most awkward part for me is trying to mask my disability by pretending I know what somebody has said, even when I don't. I'll nod my head or say something neutral like "oh" or "uh-huh," making sure the "huh" part doesn't come off as a question. I should just come clean with everyone I'm talking to, explaining how I'll need a few more repetitions before the comprehension light bulb ignites in my head.

Background noise creates havoc, and it doesn't require the interruption of anything as dramatic as a jet. If I'm standing outside, simple traffic noise from the street can undermine my hearing, as can the collective conversation of an animated group of people talking together in the same room. Background music does it too, and the sad thing is that I love music, even when the singers mash the words to their lyrics.

Once again, I'm sounding like my father-in-law. This struggle with hearing is nearly impossible to explain—the way certain sounds begin to merge, like the way "s" and "th" sounds often are indistinguishable. That moment of uncertainty is always present, when I wonder, for instance, how cutting back on the consumption of ice cream could ever make a person sin, how a drummer's use of a thimble might prove to be innovative, or how sometimes, just trying to figure out why someone said what I thought I heard them say makes me sink I am thick.

Another Chunk of Coal

The exact age when I fervently wished I owned a horse is difficult to pin down, but I suspect it was early. I remember badgering my parents about it, and I couldn't stop riding it around in my brain. It was my first full-time thought and, of course, it had to be about a horse. I spent my days from dawn to dusk thinking about it. Maybe I'd reached the age of four, or five, or even six. It doesn't matter, I guess, because that horse has been put out to pasture for more than half a century.

What's worse is that I can't remember why I so desperately wanted one. Of course, I never got a flesh-and-blood horse like the children in movies always received. Mine had the misfortune of being molded out of plastic. It stood about eight inches high with move-able legs and a saddle that could be attached, removed, and reattached by lining up little plastic pegs conveniently fitted into holes located along the top of the horse's rump.

After my parents brought the horse home for Christmas, it didn't take long for some of the pegs to break. Soon two of its legs hung limply and by New Year's Day the horse had lost its charm. I'd have shot it and put both of us out of our misery, but I had to wait until my birthday before I could convince my parents to buy me a gun.

That's how things have gone for most of my life, one blinding urge to own something followed closely by an urge to own something else. I've tried to moderate the impulse by shopping at discount stores and yard sales, but in the end I guess I'm an obsessive materialist. The philosophy that less could be more sounds good on paper, and I want to believe it, but when applied to my lifestyle the idea never works out. I also want to believe that the meek shall inherit the earth, but I suspect it will only be because all the good stuff will have been shipped to other planets.

Still, for all the bad press that consumerism generates in America, useless things have their purpose. They force me to do things I don't want to do in order to acquire them. These passions to own new things nudge me out of bed in the morning and send me off to work.

They force me to persist when it might be easier sitting back. They keep my attention focused on the world around me, the new, the innovative, the revolutionary. Ultimately, no matter what initially excites me, I always end up being the proud owner of one more useless thing.

I know it's not just me, because many friends feel the same way. The products they buy often appear to be manufactured with an eye toward their early demise. Even the plastic feels cheaper, and plastic is the main ingredient of a useless thing. Other characteristics to help define a product's uselessness include an unusually glossy finish that attracts the eye, a secret compartment for batteries, and a set of instructions that purport to be written in English.

Just to be on the safe side, a few years ago we bought a new house for Christmas, and hopefully it will be our last. The old place—which included a barn—was purchased by people who have horses, real ones. I sorted through stuff we'd gathered for over ten years, emptying shelves and drawers, digging deep into closets, and packing boxes that needed to be hauled to the new place. Moving is both an exercise in winnowing and an illustration of habit. Not surprisingly, as I agonized over what needed to be discarded, I also realized the majority of the paraphernalia I sorted through belonged not to us but to me.

The new house, only ten years old, is in good shape, although plastic is also one of its components. Maybe as we get older our toys just grow larger. What has captured my imagination is the thought that before we moved in there was a brief window of time when the new house stood empty. How convenient to think that a house—any house —is just waiting to be filled.

My wife and I agreed *not* to give each other presents that year, despite the fact that all through the holiday season we were wrapping up boxes and opening them again at a new location. I gifted myself with the stuff I couldn't bring myself to cast off, but I also pretended that everything I unpacked was a new toy, a wish fulfilled, and let's see how long that fantasy will last.

PATHOLOGICAL PUNISHMENT

We've been told in no uncertain terms that PCP plastic is bad for you and that PPE is good, especially for health workers, if only they had an adequate supply. I wonder what's up with PPO and PPV. The problem with acronyms is that they're only meaningful when the letters make sense as words. Please don't despair, because I want to talk about PP.

A Proper Pun secretes the heady aroma of an intoxicant, and it can catch the reader, listener, or even the speaker by surprise, prompting a wry smile, an outrageous laugh, or a resounding groan, like those from my brother and sister, and even from my nephew who has groaned considerably since I first held him in my arms. Now my nephew is an adult and his head is filled with wordplay. When he stands with his hands in his pockets and speaks, we listen carefully, suspecting the puns are in his genes.

People who live with people who pathologically pepper the air with puns may start to feel a little pun-shy when in the punster's presence, because there's always the expectation that each pun will be preceded by a drum roll. Mind you, I'm not accusing my nephew of anything tacky. Actually, I blame myself. I may have set a reckless example, and if I have, I apologize. Not to him, but those around him.

The best advice I can offer to pro-pun advocates, who stipple the air around them with droplets of spontaneously silly word choice, is to wear a mask because, while it can't prevent the puns from coming out, it may provide a convenient escape if no one can identify the punster when the groans start rumbling.

Ideally, the punster slips the pun into the conversation without calling attention to the mischief, because a good pun, like a good bottle of wine, is only appreciated once it's uncorked. Bragging about it only obligates the imbibers to say something nice, or worse, to say nothing at all.

I try to be discrete, because I love watching faces after I launch a pun just to see if anyone catches it. As a public-school teacher, I also punished my students by using them as an assessment tool, because offering an occasional pun helped me keep track of who might still be listening. Sometimes a student or even a stranger would look at me and raise an eyebrow, tapping a foot, or smiling. In my mind that was and is high praise, because the listener is playing the same game I'm playing, watching to see if anyone else gets it. Often the conversation just moves along, as if I meant something completely sensible, and with me it's always hard to tell.

My nephew has revealed a genuine talent for slipping an original and spontaneous pun into a conversation, but I worry he'll end up feeling like I did once, afraid he really shouldn't have spoken up. Dear nephew, if you worry too much about what you're going to say next, your vocabulary reflex will become constipated. It's important to remain open to what may come out each and every time you're sitting on the precipice of a pun.

Freud said puns are "cheap" which likely inspired a punster to write, "A Freudian slip is when you say one thing and mean your mother." Supposedly, puns have been ridiculed as the lowest form of humor, which prompted Henry Erskine to add, "...it is therefore the foundation of all wit." They are as old as language itself, having a long and respectable history, from Homer to Chaucer and Shakespeare at the respectable end of literary tradition. But every obscure journalist who crafts a punny headline for a news story redeems the modern world with another glimpse of wit. You don't have to be "literary" to turn the lowly pun into the pinnacle of repartee. If nothing else, using puns proves you're at least paying attention to what someone else is saying.

My nephew possesses an added advantage when speaking. He's nearly six-and-a-half feet tall. People around him will always be looking up to him no matter what he says. It's frosting on the cake that he can raise the level of language awareness around him even if he occasionally happens to turn out a rather mediocre pun. We all do.

One additional characteristic that makes puns so appealing is that besides having the potential to be funny, they generally present a kind of humor not grounded in racism, sexism, crudity, or just plain nastiness for the sake of a cheap laugh. I dare not categorically state that all puns are politically correct, but I will step out into the traffic of public opinion to say they are politically smart. For example, which president will always be known for his absolute incompetence? I don't know what you first thought, but if you guessed Useless S. Grant, that's exactly what I mean.

CURVES AND MITIGATION

The idea of having a window into the next fifty years sounded sort of visionary. Don't we all yearn for a closer look into the future?

I called the masked volunteer over to the display case and asked if she would show me the calendar. She scrutinized the glass shelves, then glanced up to scrutinize me.

"Did I hear you right?" she asked. "I don't see any calendar."

"Actually," I said, "it's not a paper calendar. There, on the middle shelf, that strange stainless-steel disc bearing a remarkable resemblance to the top tier of the Starship Enterprise. The little box next to it advertises it as a calendar." I pointed at it. Her expression broadened into a smile of recognition. "I'm just curious to see if it works like a crystal ball and what it might reveal about our future," I added.

"Oh, I see," she said, and now that we were on the same metaphorical stretch of road traveling in the same direction, she lifted the object and its empty cardboard container to the counter, then stepped ever so slightly back, as if shielding herself from it, or possibly from me.

At the center of the device, within the border of a tiny circle, gracefully etched letters and numbers displayed these words, FOR 50 YRS 2018-2067. A rather uninspired prophecy revealed itself to me. On the last day of 2066, I'd be 113 years old. Anyone could accurately predict where I'd be spending that New Year's Eve, which in case anyone's wondering happens to fall on a Friday. There. Something I didn't know. I also speculated that much of the world's work force, released from quarantine, would be enjoying a long holiday weekend. Just a few more revelations and I might be regarded as a soothsayer.

I bought the calendar, for no other reason than the prospect of simply touching the next fifty years, which might feel like owning a time machine.

Then, I thought about our most famous prognosticator, Nostradamus. Nobody could accuse him of fostering a cheerful disposition. His predictions read like a sustained nightmare. Take a peek into his prophecy for our 2020 political world:

In the city of God, there will be a great thunder. Two brothers are torn apart by Chaos, while the fortress endures. The great leader will succumb.

The third big war will begin when the big city is burning. It's more than a stretch to expect that anything reassuring would come from such a disclosure, but I reasoned that "the fortress endures" sounded like a shred of good news. I won't go on to repeat his other dreadful predictions involving a plague-like epidemic, an impending financial crisis, or any number of climate-related disasters, but as I studied the Nostradamus legacy, I spotted a glimmer of hope, a poetic reason for feeling less depressed. You see, all his predictions were written in rhyming quatrains. What if I set one of my own prophecies to a hip-hop beat? Might people of the future cringe less when speculating about their destiny?

As the midnight hand spasms on the brink of twelve clicks

In a distant decade of twenty-sixty-six,
A young accountant will suddenly remember
It's time to update his great grandpa's calendar.

Readers may have difficulty hearing the music, but the rhythm soothes. While it is encouraging to know I'll never need to buy another calendar to keep track of my days, it's also irresistible—with so many future months held open—to get hung up on what might happen instead of focusing on what is happening. I don't expect to live forever, but how counterproductive was it that Nostradamus never appeared to have a good night's sleep. Just look what he left for us—a divination of doom to infect our expectations nearly five hundred years after his death. For that, he should be dubbed "the coronavirus of prophets."

By way of full disclosure, my new calendar is not a crystal ball. It's just an object, about three inches in diameter and a half-inch thick. My days never fit so neatly into the palm of my hand. The brushed stainless steel surface gleams on my desktop each morning when sunlight filters through the window, so I pretend the instrument is solar powered, although it contains no electronics. Simply rotate the top disc with my finger and align the current month with its corresponding year. It's a delicate operation, one that can inadvertently add twenty years if I bump the device while getting my desktop organized. But if I'm lucky, I nudge it in the opposite direction and it makes me a little younger. That's the thing about the future, it's touchy. I can't scribble date reminders on it or hang it from a wall. But weighing in at five and a half ounces, it functions like a small rock, preventing my papers from blowing off the desk when the window gets opened. Ah, good old primitive reliability, that's the kind of prophetic assistance we all can use.

TOUR DE FARCE

Most readers are familiar with the phrase tour de force, which identifies a feat displaying great strength, skill, or ingenuity. A tour de farce, however, is quite different, referring to an empty or patently ridiculous proceeding, act, or situation that prompts a person to smile, hopefully even to laugh after the individual safely survives its circumstances.

So conjure up this dilemma: Returning home from a camping trip, I failed to use sufficient force to properly seat the ball mount into the hitch coupler on our little Scamp trailer. At highway speed thirty miles down the road, a bump disengaged the trailer from the vehicle. If not for the attached safety chains, it would have careened off the road into a ditch like a produce wagon full of watermelons, possibly flipping the vehicle with it. Instead, the tongue dropped and hung by its chains slightly above the pavement, bouncing, glancing off the road surface, igniting a trail of sparks. Let's just say the entire incident scared the hell out of me!

Absurdity pops up in everyone's life like a jack-in-the-box, but if I'm distracted— especially in matters of the heart—I forget to pay attention. Adults blame youthful inexperience for foolish behavior, while young people think slipping along the gradual downslope toward Medicare explains it all. In the end, life only offers a tour, be it forced or farced, a teeter-totter where the *wheee* is followed by a sudden impact when the laughter unexpectedly climbs off.

Recently, I lived on the road while my best friend and spouse underwent a laborious series of medical procedures to save her life. Nothing about the experience leaned toward farce, except for initially thinking we'd overpacked for what the medical staff predicted might be a short stay. In the end, it was five weeks before we managed to return home. Hospitals co-opted our existence, along with a near-lethal dose of worry every day about how things might turn out. I learned more about illness and treatment than any person needs to know, but now as I glance in the rearview mirror, I can appreciate how the occasional farce ultimately sustained us.

One long afternoon I stretched out on Pam's hospital bed so I could experience what she claimed might be a first organically animated mattress while she visited the bathroom. It wiggled and sagged and adjusted itself continuously under my weight. As I settled in, a cicada-like buzzing came to life and my right hip started rising without me having to flex a muscle. But it rose in such an awkward way I feared it might toss me out of bed and onto the floor.

Over my head, where spiritual help allegedly resides, a single ceiling tile shouted in bold letters, CALL, DON'T FALL, but I misread the message, thinking it said CRAWL, DON'T FALL. Color, text size, and positioning directly above the bed made it impossible for any patient to claim she hadn't noticed the directive. Even with my eyes closed, the words seared themselves like a branding iron into my memory.

To complement the effectiveness of this three-word commandment, an alarm installed on the bed could not be turned off by anyone except a nurse who knew the secret passcode. If a patient stood up absentmindedly, the bed erupted into such an audible commotion a visitor might think a fire alarm had just been pulled, so when Pam returned from the bathroom we repeated with the stealth of Indiana Jones in the Temple of Doom her carefully choreographed simultaneous exchange of positions, and I crawled off the bed toward the safety of a nearby chair.

People normally receive their nutritional needs from fruits and vegetables, but while in hospital Pam's surgeon prescribed enormous nasty-tasting pills, one to which she was allergic and that burned a meteoric path down her throat and esophagus, swelling her face and throat. She complained but her physician insisted.

"Couldn't I just eat bananas for my potassium?" she asked.

The surgeon replied, "You'd have to eat a thousand bananas to equal what's in one of those pills."

Eventually she said no, she wasn't taking the pills and the only thing she would miss was the swelling. The surgeon looked puzzled until she added that they made her face puff up so much her wrinkles disappeared, and then he burst out into a hearty laugh, the kind of laugh only a heart surgeon can appreciate.

I could tell you, too, about how Pam managed to turn the collapsible barf bag into a waterproof sleeve to cover her fresh stitches before taking a shower, or how her midline port for IV transfusions—one that had stayed stubbornly in place for over a month—simply fell out of her arm on the day of her discharge. Everything about this woman's sense of humor in the face of a potential disaster might keep a reader smiling, but you'd have to have been there to appreciate the *wheee* of it all.

THE URINAL'S TALE

The ring glittered like a handheld star, its opal on fire with a radiance pulsing from within the stone. I'd found a box that fit such a tiny present, and I'd even sliced a piece of foam with my pocketknife to fit the box, so the ring would perch inside it like a professional jeweler might have had it displayed, all this without a jeweler's price tag.

Then, I sketched my own greeting card with stick figures and I crafted a pun-nishingly romantic sentiment for the panel. I was new to this writing business and our marriage was still in its formative years, but I am happy to report the tradition of giving each other tacky cards has persisted now for over forty Valentine's Days. The year of the ring might have been number three or number six. I'm not sure. I certainly don't remember what I wrote, but I know the stick figures were naked and doing something slightly naughty, a style that was received so well the first time I tried that it, too, has become a tradition.

Over the years, Pam saved the cards in a shoebox she stashes, let's just say, in a place I hope no one ever discovers. And don't ask her where. She has sworn an oath that if I die first, she'll bury the whole lot. Should she go first, I'll toss them on the pyre even before I nudge her casket in.

There's just one other detail about this early romance I was hesitant to mention at the time: I'd found the ring in a urinal at the high school where I taught English. Some teenager, I presume, had broken up with his girlfriend and tossed it in, in disgust, a fairly expensive but apparently disposable token of their love. I finished, flushed, and lifted it out with my toothpick. I couldn't believe my luck! And if you can't go on reading unless I add this, then yes, I threw the toothpick away.

"This is beautiful!" was the first thing Pam said when she opened the present. "Wherever did you find it?"

I still believe that love should be grounded by honesty, but as she slipped the ring on her finger back then, a hundred lies lined up in my head like mercenary soldiers, ready to storm love's citadel. They were simply waiting for orders.

"Would you believe I found it?"

She nodded. I was, after all, the same guy who crushes aluminum cans for recycling, buys his clothing at charity shops, has never purchased a new car, and carefully opens packages he receives so as to reuse the wrapping paper or carton. The guy who once strapped a three-drawer dresser (missing one drawer) he'd found beside an alley dumpster to the back of his 750cc Kawasaki motorcycle and hauled it home, all the way from Durango. What could be that unusual about finding a ring?

I hoped she'd just accept it as another found thing, one of the mysteries of love. Nobody should have to understand love like a science. There are no proofs, only hypotheses. Every day is a further investigation.

I pictured myself at that moment as a modern-day Chaucer, narrating the urinal's tale, while we pilgrimaged down a muddy lane. Not a pretty picture. And if the public could see what Valentine's Day looks like at any public high school, parents would lock their children up. It's really part farce, part drama, but mostly exaggerated desire followed by disappointment. From the opening bell to the closing bell, the secretaries' office is crammed with floral deliveries, cards, candy, and stuffed animals, all waiting to be received by anxious and unsuspecting hearts.

At least one boy at the high school where I worked would not be having a happy Valentine's Day. Due to more than sanitary circumstances, his identity and his tragic story have been hidden from me, which is likely what he prefers.

I could have, maybe should have, let the question of where I had found it go, buried the entire thing under a metaphorical bushel basket, and moved on toward a passionate embrace, but I decided to use the same approach that has served me for four decades—the truth.

"Okay," I said, "perhaps there's something you should know before you get too attached to the ring."

"Is it a long story?"

"Yes, and a dirty one at that."

ACKNOWLEDGEMENTS

A grateful *thank you* to the editors and staff at these publications, where many of the essays collected in *Feelasophy* previously appeared: Missy Votel of the *Durango Telegraph*; Gail Binkly of the *Four Corners Free Press*, and Betsy Marston of *High Country News*. The wonderful cover watercolor is by P. Smith, also known as Pam.

ABOUT THE AUTHOR

David Feela has published three books of poetry, *Thought Experiments* (The Maverick Press, 1998), *The Home Atlas* (WordTech Editions, 2009), and *Little Acres* (Unsolicited Press, 2018). His earlier essay collection, *How Delicate These Arches* (published by Raven's Eye Press, 2011), was a finalist for the Colorado Book Award. He lives in Cortez, Colorado. His website can be excavated at davidfeela.com.

www.ingramcontent.com/pod-product-compliance
Lightning Source LLC
Chambersburg PA
CBHW070553100426
42744CB00006B/262